# PLAY WITH YOUR BRAIN

A Guide to Smarter Soccer

for

Players, Coaches, and Parents

Travis Norsen

ISBN: 978-1-7345280-0-8 (paperback)

ISBN: 978-1-7345280-2-2 (hardback)

Cover design by Seth Gregory: https://SethGregoryDesign.com

Send inquiries about bulk orders to info@pigpugpress.com.

Pig
Pug
Press

https://pigpugpress.com

To my parents:

Thank you for investing

your energy and money and time

so I could fall in love with

this beautiful game.

# Contents

# Preface

*"Football is a game you play with your brain."*

- Johan Cruyff

BECOMING a great soccer player is not easy. You have to work really hard at practice, find time to develop your individual ball skills between practices, and keep yourself in good condition (for example, by eating healthy food, stretching, and getting enough sleep) to avoid injuries and perform at the highest possible level in games.

But that is only the physical side of things. As noted by Johan Cruyff (a Dutch superstar who played for Ajax and Barcelona in the 1970s and later became a successful and influential philosopher-coach), the most important part of your body in soccer is not your feet or your legs but your brain.

There is a mental side to playing any sport. But soccer (which, outside of America, everybody just calls "football") is somewhat unique in this respect. Compared, for example, to baseball or American football, where each player has a specific job to do in a given situation, your job in soccer is less rigidly scripted. For example, if you're playing shortstop in baseball, and there are no runners on base, and the ball gets hit to you on the ground, your job is to scoop it up and throw it to the first baseman. Or, in American football, if you're playing wide receiver, your job is to run the route the quarterback assigns to you in the huddle, and catch the ball if it's thrown to you.

But what should you do when the ball comes to you in soccer? There's no one specific thing that is always right to do, even in a given type of situation. Sometimes you should dribble, sometimes you should pass, and sometimes you should shoot. But if you're going to dribble, which way should you go? Sometimes dribbling forward is the best option, but sometimes what's needed is to dribble sideways or backwards. And, if you do start dribbling in a certain direction, how far should you go before changing directions, or passing, or taking a shot?

Indeed, you even need to continuously choose what to do when you don't have the ball. For example, if your teammate is dribbling forward, should you run out in front of her and try to get into a position where you're open for a pass and can maybe score? Or should you instead drop back into a more defensive position in case she loses the ball and the other team launches a counter-attack?

Every sport requires some off-the-ball decision-making, but in terms of both the range of possibilities that are reasonable to consider in a given situation, and the continuity of its action, soccer is unique. A baseball shortstop might have to decide whether to shift left or right a couple of steps when a new batter comes to the plate. But our soccer player has to decide between sprinting forward 30 yards and sprinting backward 30 yards. And unlike baseball, where there is a pause in the action every few seconds during which players can make decisions (often with input from coaches) about these small tweaks, the decision-making in soccer has to happen during the uninterrupted flow of the game.

The point is, compared to many other sports, soccer is unusually free-form, unusually open-ended and unscripted. You have to decide, moment by moment throughout the entire game, what exactly to be doing. Yes, you need the physical skills and conditioning to actually implement your choices quickly and effectively, but if your mental decision-making is consistently poor, even the best skills and conditioning in the world won't help you.

Of course, teaching players what to do in various situations – and, in particular, how to make smart decisions both with and without the ball – is one of the main jobs of coaches. But this knowledge can be difficult and slow to develop. Not all coaches are equally good at articulating the reasons for the things they recommend. (And not all coaches recommend the right things!) Plus, no matter how good your coach might be, it is still difficult to process all of the information – which is typically shared in bits and pieces and in the heat of the moment during practice sessions and games – into a coherent, memorable whole. It is difficult, that is, to really learn the *principles* of good soccer, even from years of training sessions and games, and even from excellent coaches.

But you *need* those principles in order to make good decisions on the field. You need them in order to become the smartest – the best – soccer player you can be.

That, in a nutshell, is why I wrote this book. Its goal is simply to explain the fundamental principles of quality soccer, in a clear and organized way, and in a format that allows you to really digest them, at your own pace, far from the intensity and distractions of the training field.

If you are a player, studying the concepts in this book will give you a kind of short-cut access to a deeper understanding of the game that normally takes years (if not decades) of on-field experience to develop. It will put you in a position to consistently make better, smarter decisions on the field. It won't magically make you into a top-level player. That, unfortunately, is not something you can get from any book. So you'll still have a lot of hard work to do. But it will help you get the most out of your most important on-field weapon: your brain. In fact, I think it will help *a lot*.

I also expect the book to be of practical value for coaches. Many will learn at least a few new things, which they can pass along to their teams in various direct and indirect ways. And even for coaches who already know all of the concrete points that are covered in the book, there should be value both in its organization and in its (often novel) terminology. The title of each Chapter, for example, is a short slogan which I have found helpful in communicating with my team, as a summary of the principle which that Chapter analyzes and illustrates. Note also that I have included, at the end, an Appendix for Coaches which describes some training activities that I have found to be particularly effective at reinforcing the principles covered in the book.

Finally, I expect the book to be of interest to soccer moms and dads, who invest tons of time and energy (and money) making it possible for their kids to pursue their passion for the sport. (Thank you for that, by the way.) This book will give you a deeper insight into what your kids are (or should be) learning, and might even help you help them get better. (Someday they may even thank you for that themselves.)

To summarize, if you want to understand soccer better – so you can make smarter decisions and learn to play at a higher level, or so you can become a more effective coach, or so you can better support your own kids' interest in the sport – I wrote this book for you.

Before jumping in, here are a few nuts-and-bolts things you should understand about how the book works.

First, I have tried to write in a somewhat interactive style. In particular, I regularly pose questions and invite you to pause and develop your own thoughts on a certain topic before you read on and hear mine. My day-job is teaching physics, and my experience there tells me that you will learn more, and have an easier time applying your knowledge later, if you really do pause and reflect, before reading on, at these points. If your answer ends up being the same as the one I think is correct, it will reinforce your confidence in the relevant concept. And if your answer ends up being different from the one I endorse, your having genuinely thought about the question and committed to an answer on the basis of some reasoning, will make you more receptive to hearing my alternative point of view. If, in the end, you agree with me (and you might not always do so, and that's OK!) you'll have the experience of really seeing something new. The point in question will stick more deeply than it would if you were just nodding along to another thing somebody says.

Second, the book contains more than fifty diagrams to illustrate and explain the concepts in a clear, visual way. These pictures are essential, but so is the text. So please resist the temptation to either read the paragraphs but gloss over the pictures and their captions, or vice versa. (Different people with different learning and reading styles are sometimes tempted in one or the other of these two directions.) And when the text refers to a diagram, take the time to flip back or ahead, if needed, to look at it right then, even if it is a page or two (or even several chapters) away.

Third, because the team I am currently coaching plays 9v9 (i.e., nine players on the field at a time) most of the diagrams which show everyone (or almost everyone) on the pitch assume a 9v9 game. (Our team, the white circles in all of the diagrams, typically play a 3-4-1, while the opponents, the black triangles, typically play a 3-3-2, for what it's worth.) But all of the ideas in the book are equally applicable whether you play 9v9, 7v7, 11v11, or whatever. That is, the focus is always on the conceptual principles involved in some pattern of play, not on any formation-specific issue about who, exactly, should be performing some particular job.

That said, there are some cases where the words used to describe a certain player would be different in a different game-size or different formation. For example, the roles of (what I describe as) our outside backs and wings (in the context of a 9v9 game in a 3-4-1 shape) might, respectively, be played instead by the center backs and outside backs in a 4-back system (such as a 4-3-1 or 4-4-2). I don't think this issue should cause much trouble, but you should be aware going in that although every team will want and need someone to do the things we talk about, the name of the position assigned to a certain task may well be different on your team.

Finally, here is how the diagrams work. There are two teams. Your team is the "white circles" and the opponents are the "black triangles." You are usually one particular player on the white circles team. Your teammates are just generic white circles, but you are special: you have eyes, arms, and two feet. So here, for example, is what it looks like when you are standing on the left, waving at two of your teammates, with a black triangle player (with a ball) behind them:

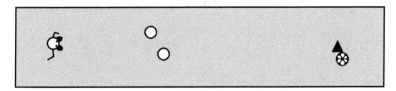

Your team (the white circles) is always trying to score in the goal that is at the top of the figure (which I will occasionally describe as the "north" end to avoid ambiguity) and defend the goal that is at the bottom (the "south" end). The path of the ball is always shown with dashed lines (which are straight for on-the-ground passes and curved for up-in-the-air long balls), while the movements of players are indicated with solid lines or curves. When someone is *dribbling* with the ball, that is indicated with a solid zig-zag type line. And, finally, things happening now (or in the immediate future) are typically shown in black and white, whereas things in the past are (when shown) shown in gray.

So, for example, if you had the ball on the left wing (facing to the right), then passed it to a teammate near the middle of the field, and then ran forward (past a stationary black triangle defender) to receive it (while now facing forward), and now you're about to dribble forward toward the goal, that would look like this:

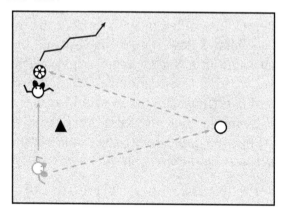

OK, you get it and you are ready to rock. Let's jump in!

# CHAPTER 1

---

# Possession Is Precious

*"There is only one ball, so you need to have it."*

- Johan Cruyff

EVERYONE who has played soccer has had the unpleasant experience of getting completely destroyed by a superior team. Here is how it typically goes. They bring the ball down, you and your teammates work your butts off to try to keep them from scoring, maybe you do eventually win the ball from them and try to go forward, but inevitably your team loses it near midfield and has to scramble to get back on defense as the other team begins yet another attack.

It's both physically and mentally exhausting to have to switch, over and over again, from hopeful forward movements (dribbling forward or running forward to get open for a forward pass) to sprinting backwards to get back in position to defend after your team turns the ball over. As this cycle continues, you eventually become so tired and demoralized that you either give up on moving forward when your team does win the ball, or give up on recovering backwards when your team loses the ball. But if nobody goes forward when your team has the ball, you have no chance of scoring, and you'll just end up letting the other team win the ball back even closer to the goal you're defending. And if people on your team do go forward when you get the ball, but are then too exhausted to get back on defense when you lose it, the other

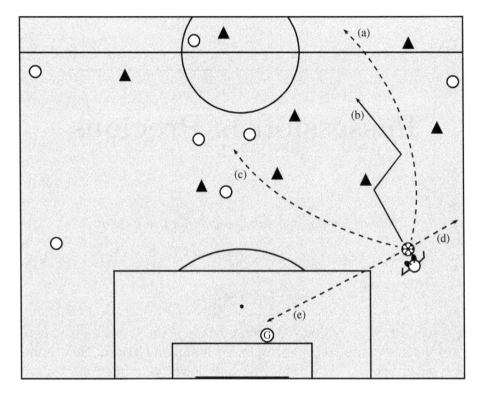

*Figure 1A: The goalie passes the ball to you, the right back, in the situation shown. Your options include: (a) booting the ball downfield as far as possible with the hope that your forward or winger will get there first, (b) trying to dribble forward through the opposing players, (c) passing it toward the middle where several of your teammates are congregated, (d) kicking it straight out of bounds, and (e) passing immediately backwards to the goalie who just passed it to you. What do you think is the smartest decision?*

*The dashed lines and curves in the Figure represent, respectively, on-the-ground and in-the-air trajectories of the ball. The solid zig-zag represents you dribbling with the ball. See the last couple pages of the Preface for a more detailed explanation of how this and future Figures work.*

team can now attack with a numbers advantage and probably score.

The end result, of course, is that your team loses by a lot, and has a pretty miserable time doing it.

And so the question is: how can you break out of that cycle or, better yet, avoid getting into it in the first place?

Let's get into discussing that with a pop quiz! Imagine that you are the right back in the situation depicted in Figure 1A: the other team takes a long shot from about 30 yards in front of the goal, your goalie easily stops it with her feet because there's no pressure on her, and she passes the ball out to you. What should you do?

(a) Boot the ball forward as hard as you can and hope that your forward can get to it first.

(b) Dribble forward and try to beat the defenders and score.

(c) Kick the ball toward the crowd near the center of the field since several of your teammates are there.

(d) Kick the ball out of bounds since there are no really good forward passing options and your team needs some time to recover its defensive positioning.

(e) Pass the ball right back to your goalie as quickly as possible.

Before reading on, take a couple of minutes to look carefully at the Figure, think about the different options, and decide what you think you should do.

I'll give you one more minute to think about what you'd do and why, and then we can compare answers. I'll share my thoughts on all five of the possibilities, starting with the one I think is the very worst.

So, option (c) has you kicking the ball into the middle of the field. You have three teammates there, so it might seem likely that one of them will manage to get the ball. And it's true that, if they do, it puts your team into a pretty good position to move forward and create a goal-scoring opportunity. But your pass could also easily be intercepted by a black triangle player who would then be able to dribble, basically uncontested, at your goal. So there's a really good chance that option (c) will lead to a quick goal by the other team. The pass is just too risky.

Option (b), dribbling forward, is also pretty risky. If that first black triangle player gets the ball away from you, she will be able to dribble unimpeded at your goal and probably score. And even if you get past the first black triangle player, several more will squeeze into your dribbling lane and pressure you. If you are fast and have good ball skills, there's an excellent chance you can dribble past a single defender. But even the most skilled players are extremely unlikely to take on four defenders and make it out the other side with the ball. So since the result of losing the ball is potentially catastrophic, option (b) is also just not very good.

What about option (d), kicking the ball out of bounds? Compared to the turnovers that are likely to result with options (c) and (b), this at least gives the other team the ball in a less dangerous place – over on the sideline, far from the goal, instead of closer to the middle of the field in front of the goal. And if you kick the ball *way* out of bounds, your team will get a few seconds to catch its breath and recover its defensive shape before the next attack comes. So option (d) is less risky, compared to options (c) and (b), but still pretty bad since you are just giving away the ball and allowing the other team to start that next attack.

Although it might seem far superior to some, option (a) – booting the ball downfield – is actually not that different from option (d). Of course, the hope with option (a) is that your forward or winger will get to the ball first and maybe have a chance to dribble down and score. But the three players closest to where the ball lands are black triangles, so it's extremely unlikely that one of your teammates will get to the ball first. Option (a) is therefore really just a slightly different way of giving the ball back to the other team. It's true that, like kicking the ball *way* out of bounds, booting it downfield gives you a few seconds to breathe and get in position to defend the next attack. And if the other team is going to start an attack, it's probably a little better to make them start it from near midfield, than from the sideline closer to your goal. So maybe option (a) is a slightly better way of giving the ball back to the other team, compared to option (d). But only slightly.

Note that all of the options we've considered so far have one thing in common: they are likely to result in turnovers. Exactly how bad these options are, relative to each other, depends on two factors: how likely they are to result in turnovers, and how likely the other team is to score if a turnover does occur.

But setting these details aside, the crucial point is that options (a), (b), (c), and (d) are all bad – bad because they involve giving the ball back to the other team and hence guaranteeing that the black triangles come at your team with yet another exhausting, demoralizing attack.

Let's then finally consider option (e), passing the ball right back to the goalie who just passed it to you. In my opinion this is the best of the five options. And it is not just the least bad of five bad options. It is the only option that is positively and unambiguously *good*.

Why is it good? Well, for one, of all of your teammates who are close enough that you could reasonably try to pass to them, your goalie is the most wide open. That means there's no risk that the pass will be intercepted, and it means that when the goalie gets the ball she'll have plenty of time to make a smart decision about what to do with it. Of course, it's pretty obvious what she should do with it: pass the ball to the one teammate who is even *more* wide open than the goalie, namely, the left back! This would put your team in a really strong position to start moving forward, with acres of space and tons of time. This means you get to dictate the play for a while, move downfield as a unit, and the black triangles (who are now mostly on the wrong side of the field!) have to work their butts off to get back into position and defend. Option (e) is the way to break out of the cycle of demoralizing exhaustion and give your team the best chance to build toward a scoring opportunity.

But this raises an important question: if option (e) is so good, why do so many players, in situations like the one depicted in the Figure, never do it?

In many cases, the unfortunate answer is: because playing the ball backwards – and to their own goalie of all things! – makes their parents and/or coaches yell at them with horror and outrage. But that doesn't really answer the question. *Why* are so many people – both players and the adults who influence them – so obsessed with making the ball go forward? I guess the answer is that they want to win the game, which requires scoring goals, which requires getting the ball all the way forward.

But this way of thinking about soccer is just wrong. The whole point of the pop quiz is that "going forward" in various direct, simple-minded ways – e.g., by dribbling the ball into a crowd of defenders in front of you, or kicking it forward as far as you can without any thought about what will happen to it after it gets there – are not actually good ways of moving the ball downfield and generating a goal-scoring opportunity.

Getting the ball all the way forward – into the other team's net – is the ultimate goal, but you just can't accomplish it by going directly toward it in a straight line. I am reminded here of Doc Hudson's advice to Lightning McQueen (in the classic Disney/Pixar movie, "Cars"): if you want to stay on the road, when it bends sharply to the left, you need to turn the steering wheel hard to the *right*. Turning right to go left sounds paradoxical and Lightning McQueen responds with sarcastic dismissiveness:

> "Oh, right. That makes perfect sense. Turn right to go left. Yes, thank you! Or should I say 'No, thank you' because in Opposite World, maybe that really means thank you."

But when he tries it out, he finds that Doc Hudson was exactly right.

It is the same way in soccer. Often you have to go backwards to go forwards. Moving forward is the long-range goal, but maintaining possession of the ball is the only consistently reliable way to achieve that goal. And maintaining possession of the ball means you have to be willing to make the easy pass, to a teammate who will have more time and more space and better forward-progress options, even if that teammate is behind you.

In short: *Possession is precious.*

We've been thinking about this principle in the context of the situation depicted in Figure 1A. But the idea applies much more generally, and the principle has some other implications that weren't touched on above. Let's expand on a few of these points.

## 1.1 ⚽ Never just "boot it"

As illustrated with option (a) in the Figure 1A scenario, blasting the ball forward to nobody in particular usually results in a turnover. This is a bad thing. So you should never do it. Instead, take that extra second to get your composure, look up, identify an open teammate, and pass the ball to her. If that open teammate happens to be behind you, don't sweat it. Sometimes you have to go backwards to go forwards.

This rule deserves a couple of follow-ups. First, it does occasionally happen that the ball is loose right in front of your goal, or is rolling toward an open net, and there is no time to do anything but just clear it away as fast and as far as possible. In a true emergency situation like that, of course it is fine to just "boot it" away to relieve the immediate danger.

That having been said, though, the threat level is rarely as high as it feels in the moment. (Overly-anxious coaches and parents yelling "Clear!!" or "AWAY!!!" generally don't help here.) Great players learn how to avoid panicking, keep their composure even in front of their own goal, and convert a dangerous situation into possession for their team, instead of just a slightly-less-dangerous situation. Of course, you're bound to make some mistakes and some of those mistakes might lead to goals for the other team. That's fine. To develop calm, confident composure on the ball, you have to make some mistakes and learn from them. My advice is: have that learning experience while you're still young!

Second, note that the "never just 'boot it'" rule applies to everybody on the team – including the goalie. Way too often (in American youth soccer at least) goalies are trained to punt the ball whenever they get it in their hands, or blast it forward (to nobody in particular) with their first touch if it ever comes to them on the ground. But just like option (a) from earlier, this almost always results in a turnover near midfield. This is a bad thing. So you should never do it. And coaches and parents should never encourage it. If there is a teammate near midfield who is so open that you (the goalie) can get it to her, with high probability, by punting or blasting the ball that way, then by all means go for it. But if (as is much more commonly the case) opposing players outnumber your teammates in the area near midfield, then you should do just what everybody else on the team should do: take that extra second to get your composure, look up, figure out which teammate is the most open, and throw/pass/punt the ball to her so your team can keep possession.

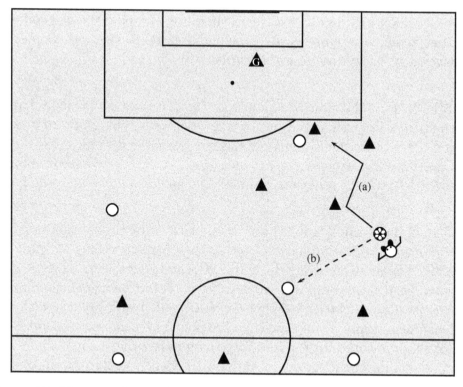

*Figure 1B: You are playing forward and receive the ball in your offensive end. But there are several defenders between you and the goal. Should you (a) try to dribble through them, or (b) pass backwards to an open teammate?*

## 1.2 ⚽ Don't dribble into trouble

Option (b) from Figure 1A was meant to illustrate the danger of trying to dribble the ball, through traffic, out of your own defensive end. This is particulary risky because, if the other team takes the ball away from you, they might be able to score a quick goal. But what if, say, you're a forward and you receive the ball down past midfield, in your own offensive end? See Figure 1B. Is it a good idea to dribble forward in this situation?

Take a minute to look at the Figure and think about what you'd do in this situation.

Here's what I would say. Dribbling forward in the Figure 1B situation is certainly less risky than it would be in the 1A situation. If you lose the ball in your offensive end of the field, it doesn't put your team in immediate danger of being scored on, the way it does in your defensive end.

But dribbling forward is still not a good idea, even in this less risky situation. If it's unlikely for you to successfully dribble through four defenders, then trying to do so, no matter how far away from your own goal you are, is just another way of gifting the ball to the other team. But that's a bad thing. So you should never do it. Instead, recognize that the immediate path forward is clogged, find an open teammate with better options in front of her, and pass the ball to her as quickly as possible.

There are only a certain fixed number of defenders on the other team, so if the path between you and the goal is clogged, that means there are some really good attacking opportunities somewhere else on the field. Help the ball find them so your team can exploit them!

## 1.3 ⚽ Don't just kick it out of bounds

You probably thought that option (d) in the Figure 1A scenario – just kicking it straight out of bounds – was a bit strange. Would anyone really do this, or even consider doing this? I admit, I mostly included it so I could explain that (despite being a rather obviously bad idea) it's probably better than options (b) and (c) and only marginally worse than option (a). But it's true that, unlike the other options, (d) isn't something I see kids doing very often.

However, there is a very similar situation in which I see kids just deliberately kick the ball out of bounds all the time. See Figure 1C. The other team has played a ball over the top, and you, the right back, are able to get there first. But several black triangle players are hot on your heels, so it would be very dangerous to try to stop the ball, turn around, and dribble (or pass) forwards.

What should you do?

Often, in this situation, kids will just kick the ball out of bounds. This buys a few seconds for the other white circles to get back and set up a defensive structure. But of course it also just gives the ball to the other team.

Why do that? Instead, you can just pass it immediately backwards to the

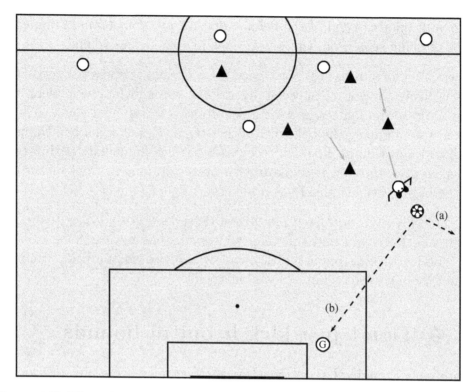

*Figure 1C: The other team just booted the ball forward past midfield and everybody is chasing it. You, the right back, are able to get to the ball first. Should you (a) kick the ball out of bounds, or (b) immediately pass it backwards to your wide-open teammate, the goalie?*

goalie, who can hold it for a second and wait for, say, the left back to get open on the other side. Any time you are faced with the choice of giving the ball to the other team, or keeping it for your team, you should keep it for your team, even if that means going temporarily backwards.

Possession is precious.

## 1.4 ⚽ Win it going backwards

A closely-related situation happens all the time in the middle of the field. An errant pass or deflection creates a loose 50/50 ball, which you and a player from the other team both have a chance of getting to first. Consider

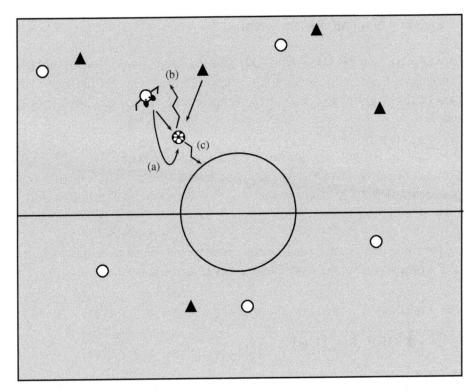

*Figure 1D: The ball is loose in the middle of the field. You and one opposing player both have a chance to get to the ball first and win it. Do you: (a) take a curved approach to the ball so you will be going forward when you get to it, (b) run straight at the ball but immediately turn forward with it, or (c) run straight at the ball and then continue going backwards with it?*

in particular the situation shown in Figure 1D: you could (a) take a curved path to the ball so that when you get to it you are going forwards, or you could (b) run straight to the ball and immediately turn and try to dribble forwards, or you could (c) run straight at the ball and continue dribbling with it in that same direction.

What do you think is the best option? After you've thought about it, read on to hear what I think.

The problem with (a), taking a curved path to the ball so you can be facing forward when you get there, is that the longer, non-direct approach makes you get there *later* – probably after the black triangle player has already arrived and won the ball for her team.

With option (b), you get there first, but immediately turn into the on-rushing black triangle player who may tackle it away from you. So neither of these first two options gives you a high probability of winning – and keeping – possession.

But with option (c) you are guaranteed to get, and keep, the ball. The fact that you get it going backwards does not make this a less desirable option! Just pass it immediately backwards to one of your open teammates and your team can start going forward from there.

Having the ball (but going backwards) is way better than a mere chance of having it (but going forwards). Possession is precious.


## 1.5 ⚽ Pass to feet

When the ball comes to you, it is much easier to control it and get ready for your next move (which might be shooting, dribbling, or passing) if it comes to your feet. Balls up in the air, which you have to try to settle with your thigh or chest or head, are much more difficult to handle.

And what's true for you is true for everyone else, too. Therefore, if you want your team to maintain possession of the ball, your passes should almost always be to a teammate's feet.

Of course, if the teammate you are passing to is running into an open space, you shouldn't pass the ball to where her feet are *now*, or she'll have to stop and turn around to go get it. Instead, pass it to where her feet will be when she receives it. That is, put it into the space she's running into – but put it there *on the ground* so she can easily control it with her feet when she gets there.

The principle is: make it as easy as possible for your teammate to control the ball by keeping your passes, whenever possible, down at foot-level. Why? You know the answer: because possession is precious.

## 1.6 ⊛ Don't cheer turnovers

This last point is mostly for parents and coaches. Far too often, I see and hear adults praising things that actually undermine the team's success. For example: a defender steals the ball away from the other team's striker, turns nicely forward with it (using her body to shield the ball from the dispossessed striker), and then promptly kicks the ball 50 yards downfield to the other team's center back – and, from the sideline, her dad yells "Nice boot Jamie!" But, do you know what it's called when a defender makes a really nice defensive play and then boots it 50 yards downfield to the other team? That's called a turnover.

Or: the most skilled player on the team gets the ball out on the right wing (like in Figure 1B), beats three consecutive defenders with an amazing display of technical brilliance, and then loses it to the fourth defender – and the coach yells "Beautiful run, Sophia!" But, again, do you know what you call it when somebody dribbles through three defenders but then loses it to the fourth? That's right, it's called a turnover.

It sounds paradoxical, but making the easy pass, to a wide-open teammate, is often very difficult. There is a constant temptation to do something big and flashy and risky instead. But good soccer requires intelligence and discipline. Adults who want to encourage good soccer should stop cheering for big flashy turnovers, and start cheering instead for sensible decisions that allow the team to keep the ball. Possession, after all, is precious.

## 1.7 ⊛ Overview

Soccer is a team sport. At the most primitive level (very young children playing small-sided games) a single talented player can "do it herself." But in bigger games with more mature and skilled players, consistently scoring goals and winning games requires the team to be able to possess the ball for reasonably long stretches of time. The team must be able to win the ball, pass it around to get out of trouble, find teammates who have time and space, move forward together into the offensive end, and eventually create a scoring opportunity.

But the team can only do those things if each individual player is committed to the value of possession. You must win loose balls for your team even if it means going backwards. You must recognize that dribbling into traffic, booting the ball forward to nobody, and kicking it out of bounds just give the ball to the other team. Pass the ball to an open teammate instead, even if that teammate is behind you. And when you do pass the ball, put your teammate in the best possible position to keep possession for your team by passing it to her feet.

Let's make all of this concrete using a little math. To generate a decent scoring opportunity, your team has to win the ball and complete some number of consecutive passes – call it $N$ – leading up to a shot on goal. How many passes will it take to create this legitimate scoring opportunity? Obviously the answer depends on lots of different factors like where on the field your team wins the ball, how many of the passes are forwards and how many are backwards, etc. But if you want your team to be able to break out of the exhausting and depressing cycle we began with, $N$ is clearly going to have to be bigger than one or two. A typical passing sequence leading to a successful goal-scoring opportunity is shown in Figure 1E: a central midfielder wins the ball (going backwards), passes it backwards to an outside back, who passes it backwards to the goalie, who swings the ball over to the outside back on the open side of the field, who passes to the forward-running center back, who puts the ball out in front of the left winger, who passes it to the other center mid, who puts the ball into the penalty area in front of the forward who runs onto it and rockets a shot into the goal at the far post. That's $N = 7$ passes (two of them backwards!) leading to a goal.

Of course this is just one possible example. The point is that consistently generating goal-scoring opportunities requires your team to be able to consistently string 5, 10, or maybe 15 passes together. If you can't do that, you won't score goals, and you won't win.

But then here is the important math. Suppose each player on the team is able to control the ball and successfully pass to a teammate with probability $p$. Then it turns out that the average number of successful passes before the first turnover is $N = \frac{p}{(1-p)}$.

So, for example, if each player has only a 50% chance of successfully completing the next pass ($p = 0.5$), then on average the team will only be able

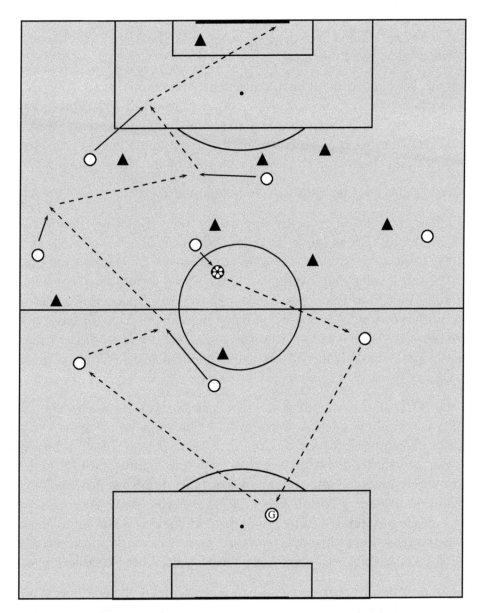

*Figure 1E: A typical successful possession, with $N = 7$ consecutive passes leading up to a shot on goal.*

to complete $N = \frac{0.5}{1.0-0.5} = \frac{0.5}{0.5} = 1$ pass before turning the ball over. That is nowhere near good enough!

What if $p = 75\%$? Then $N = \frac{.75}{1.00-.75} = \frac{.75}{.25} = 3$. That's a little better, but still nowhere near good enough!

If the team is going to be able to consistently complete about (say) $N = 9$ passes, without turning the ball over, this requires each individual player – and so, in particular, it requires *you* – to successfully complete the next pass about 90% of the time. Or equivalently, the requirement is that you turn the ball over to the other team at most about 10% of the times you get it.

You should pause and let that sink in for a minute.

The numbers here tell a crucially important story. But they should not be taken *too* literally. For example, a center back (or goalie!) who turns the ball over 10% of the time would be a complete disaster! Defenders (and goalies) need to be much safer than average, i.e., they need to aim for $p$ considerably higher than 90%. On the other hand, a striker who successfully passes the ball 90% of the time is probably playing too safely. You do have to take risks to score goals, so a striker who turns the ball over half of the time, but frequently puts the ball in the net the other half of the time, is probably doing OK.

Still, the 90% rule of thumb is a great way for you to assess the extent to which your individual play is compatible with the requirements of team possession. Keep track (or ask a coach or parent to keep track) of how many times you get the ball during a game, and how many of those end with positive outcomes (successful passes or legitimate shots on goal) as opposed to turnovers. If your $p$ is well below 90% (and you aren't scoring a ton of goals), you are absolutely killing your team! Review and start implementing the concrete tips from this chapter (e.g., pass backwards more often, stop dribbling into trouble, etc.) to bring your $p$ up into a reasonable range.

One last note. In my experience (both as a coach and a player) there is almost no correlation between a person's skill-level and her $p$ score. Sometimes, as one would expect, it is the least experienced and least skilled players who kill their team by turning the ball over way too often. But just as often it is the most skilled players who kill their team by, for example, always dribbling into traffic, maybe getting by two or three defenders with some fancy footwork, but then inevitably losing it to the third or fourth.

The lesson of this chapter is not about skill level, but attitude. Whether you are the most skilled or least skilled player on your team, you have the ability to add something to, or instead get in the way of, your team's quest to score goals and win games. Gobble up loose balls for your team and then make the easy, sensible pass to a teammate who has lots of space to work with – instead of something flashier that results in a turnover – and you'll be making a real, positive contribution to your team's success.

Good things will happen when you adopt for yourself the mindset that possession is precious!

# CHAPTER 2

---

# Yell With Your Legs

*"When you play a match, it is statistically proven that players actually have the ball 3 minutes on average ... So, the most important thing is: what do you do during those 87 minutes when you do not have the ball. That is what determines whether you're a good player or not."*

- Johan Cruyff

O NE of my biggest pet peeves as a coach is illustrated in Figure 2A: you yell for the ball even though there is a defender between it and you.

Doing this is worse than useless. With the defender in the way, it is impossible for your teammate to pass the ball to your feet. But your yelling also gets your teammate's attention, making him take the time to look up at you and recognize, in the heat of the moment, that even though you are yelling for the ball, he cannot actually pass the ball to you. Your yelling, that is, distracts him from his job of figuring out how to help the team by completing the next pass. But that job is hard enough already. By distracting him, you waste his precious time and make it more likely that he'll turn the ball over and force your whole team to retreat and play defense.

When I see a player do this, I tell them: "Yell with your legs!" This means: close your mouth and instead use your *legs* to communicate to your teammate that you want the ball. And, for the record, I do not have in mind that you should do a handstand and wave your legs back and forth in the air. Rather,

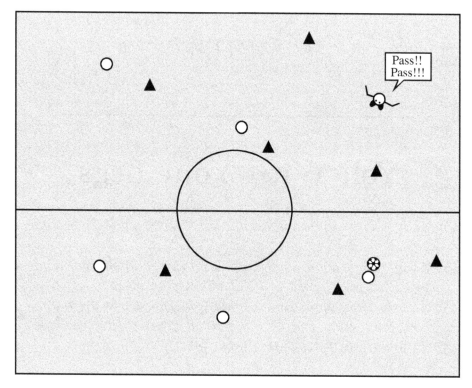

*Figure 2A: You want your teammate to pass to you, so you call for the ball even though there is a defender in the way. What are you thinking?*

I mean that you should use your legs to move your body into a position where your teammate can see that he can pass the ball to your feet. (In traditional soccer parlance, this idea of moving to get open for a pass – and in particular making your openness *visible* to your teammate with the ball – is called "showing for the ball" or just "showing.")

Yelling with your legs (i.e., showing for the ball) has several aspects which we can discuss in more detail.

## 2.1 ⚽ Seek the seam

Your teammate cannot (easily) pass the ball to your feet if there is a defender between him and you. In order to be a viable passing option, you therefore have to move into a gap – a seam – between defenders. Two good possibilities

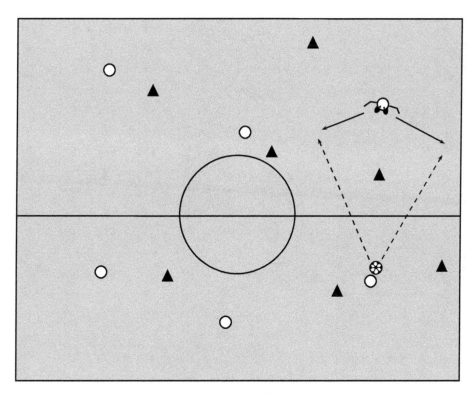

*Figure 2B: If you want the ball, move into a seam between defenders so your teammate can pass the ball to your feet without a defender intercepting it.*

are shown in Figure 2B.

This is not the most complicated idea in the world. But it does require an ongoing effort during the game, because this is not just something you should be doing every now and then. Rather, it is something you should be doing *all of the time*, whenever your team has the ball. As the ball moves around, and as the players on the other team move around in response, the locations of seams in the defense, through which a successful pass to your feet can occur, keep changing. So you have to constantly adjust your position to follow them and find new ones.

You have to actively and continuously seek the seams.

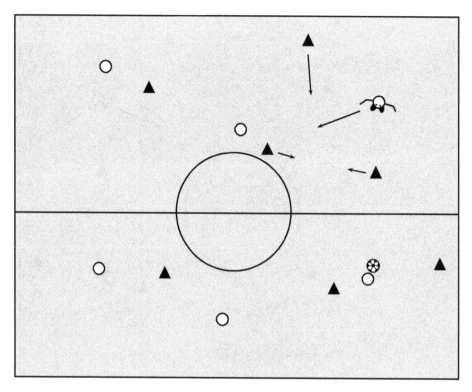

*Figure 2C: When you move into a seam, good defenders will react to try to prevent or intercept the pass to you. The two defenders on each side of the seam will squeeze in and try to pinch off the passing lane. And the deeper defender will step forward so that, if the ball is played to you, he can step in front and intercept it – or at least apply intense pressure – just as you receive it.*

## 2.2 ⚽ Move toward the ball

Often, simply moving into a seam between two defenders is enough. Your teammate with the ball sees a clear passing lane between him and you, and so he passes the ball to your feet. This works because typically defenders will be facing and watching the ball, so if you move into the seam *behind them*, as in Figure 2B, they won't even be aware that you're there and therefore won't try to close off the passing lane.

But that's really just the best case scenario. Good defenders will be aware

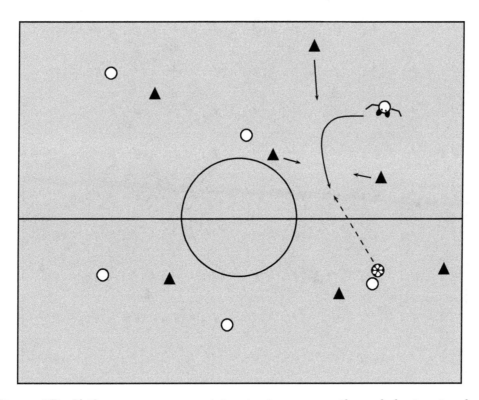

*Figure 2D: If the seam you want to receive a pass through begins to close, you can remain a viable passing option by moving toward the ball along the seam.*

of what's going on both in front of them and behind them, and/or will be facing a direction that allows them to simultaneously see not only the ball but also passing options like you. And if they recognize that a pass to you, in the seam, is about to occur, they will squeeze in and pinch off the seam, as shown in Figure 2C. In addition, there is usually at least one even-deeper defender who can see perfectly clearly what you are trying to do and who, by moving forward, can get himself into a position to step in front of you and intercept the pass or at least challenge hard for the ball as it is arriving.

In order to remain a viable passing option in the face of these defensive readjustments, it is often necessary to *move toward the ball* in the seam, as shown in Figure 2D.

Note that there is a kind of trade-off here. All other things being equal, you'd

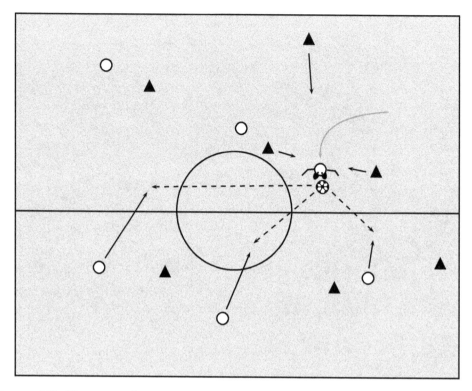

*Figure 2E: You moved toward the ball along the seam to receive the pass, so now you have it, going backwards, in the position shown. But your teammates give you lots of good passing options by moving into seams toward the ball.*

rather receive the ball in the seam *behind* the defenders. That way, when you get it, you can turn forward and have two fewer defenders to worry about getting past. But if you just move into the seam behind the two defenders and stand there, there's a good chance the defenders will pinch in and intercept the pass – or your teammate with the ball will see them pinching in, realize that the pass to you is no longer likely to succeed, and have to scramble to find some alternative option. By moving toward the ball, you might get it in a slightly less advantageous position, but at least you get (i.e., your team keeps) the ball. And, as you might have heard, possession is precious.

And note, finally, that even if you do have to sacrifice a bit of position and receive the ball going backwards in order to make the pass viable, that's not such a terrible thing. Your teammates, after all, have also studied this

Chapter so they, too, will be yelling with their legs – moving into seams and moving toward the ball – and so, as illustrated in Figure 2E, you'll have lots of good passing options that give your team opportunities to move the ball forward again.

## 2.3  ⚽  Clearing out

It might have occurred to you that, if everybody is always trying to get open by moving toward the ball, pretty soon everybody will be huddled, in a tight mass, right where the ball is. You've probably seen this happen in very young kids' soccer games. For a team that wants to be able to pass the ball around and maintain possession, it's definitely not a good look!

The next two Chapters are all about the need to maintain good spacing between players both horizontally (side to side across the field) and vertically (forward and backward along the field). So, much of our discussion of how to avoid the "kindergarten clump" can be postponed to the following Chapters.

Here I just want to put some limits on the idea of moving toward the ball to get open for a pass, to make sure it's clear that this is not something everybody should be doing all of the time.

First, as mentioned already in the last section, it is much better to receive the ball in the island of space behind the defenders, if that is a possibility. So if no pressure is coming up from behind, and the seam isn't closing, just stay put and wait for the pass in this more advantageous position. The need to move toward the ball, along the seam, only arises in a situation where (a) the ball is definitely coming and (b) you're worried that you won't end up keeping it if you just stay put.

Sometimes you'll know the ball is definitely coming because it's already on its way. Or you might recognize that your teammate with the ball is under intense pressure and has to get rid of the ball immediately, and you're his only remotely decent passing option. In these sorts of cases, moving toward the ball is the best way to give your team the best chance of keeping it.

But sometimes things play out in a different way. For example, maybe just as you start moving toward the ball, some other safer passing option opens up and your teammate with the ball turns away from you to consider this

new option. Or maybe, recognizing that all of his passing options are too
risky, your teammate turns with the ball and starts dribbling backwards to
buy himself some time.

In these sorts of cases – where your teammate with the ball communicates,
through his actions, that it's not coming to you – running toward him is no
longer appropriate. You'll just get in his way, pull defenders in, and add to
his troubles.

When this happens, you should instead clear out. Move *away* from the ball.
This creates space closer to the ball that another one of your teammates
might need to use to get open. And it puts you in a position to begin the
cycle again: make yourself available in a seam, drift toward the ball as needed
to keep the passing option alive, and then clear out when you see that you're
not going to get it.

You can think of it this way: moving toward the ball is a way of offering help
to your teammate who currently has it. Sometimes that help is desperately
needed and warmly accepted: he escapes the immediate pressure by passing
you the ball, your team keeps it, and you move on together from there. But
sometimes your teammate, though no doubt appreciating your offer to help,
doesn't think you're the best option and communicates that to you (typically
either by looking away or turning away). When that happens, you should
respect his judgment: clear out and let him get help from somebody else or
figure out how to help himself.

## 2.4  ⚽  Yelling with your mouth

The point of the slogan "Yell with your legs" is that if you aren't actively
moving around to get yourself open for a pass, you are probably not open
for a pass, and so yelling (with your mouth) for the ball just gets in the way
of your teammate's attempt to complete the next pass and thus keep your
team in possession of the ball.

But this should not be taken to mean that calling for the ball in the traditional way, with your mouth, is an inherently bad thing. In general, communication between teammates on the field is a good thing, and there's no
doubt that your mouth can be an effective communication tool if used prop-

erly. We do not want soccer players to take vows of silence like Buddhist monks.

The point is rather that calling for the ball verbally, with your mouth, has to take a secondary role. *First* you have to use your legs to move so that you are actually in a good position to receive a high-percentage pass. *Then*, if further communication is needed – for example, because your teammate with the ball hasn't seen you yet, or because you want to stress that you *really* want the ball because there's some fantastic opportunity if only he gets it to you immediately – go ahead and use your mouth.

A simple "Yes!" or "Feet!" (as in: "Pass it to my ...") usually suffices and can be very helpful, once you've done the work of actually getting yourself open.

## 2.5 ⚽ Overview

The take-home message of Chapter 1 was that many players (and coaches and parents) need to change their fundamental mindset about how soccer works. In particular, instead of thinking that the goal is always to move the ball forward, right now, as far and as fast as possible, they instead need to understand that moving the ball forward is only the long-term goal, and that the way to achieve that long-term goal is for the team to possess the ball for long stretches of time, which requires passing to the most open players whether they are forward or backward.

I have a similar paradigm-shifting message in mind here in Chapter 2.

Many beginning players (and coaches and parents) think of a soccer team as a collection of individuals who take turns trying to move the ball forward and, ideally, score a goal. In this way of thinking about the game, when somebody else on your team has the ball – when it is "their turn" – you are not really involved. So you just sit back and watch the show.

When teams that play with this mindset have the ball, one person – the guy with the ball – is working *really hard*, and everybody else is just kind of standing around passively watching him work.

But, as you might remember from Chapter 1, possession is precious. And possession requires constantly moving the ball away from pressure by passing to more-open teammates. There will only be a continuous supply of more-open teammates, though, if the people without the ball are constantly working to get, and stay, open for passes.

So there is really a fundamentally different conception here of what good team soccer should look like. The person with the ball should not be the only one working hard. Instead, all of his teammates should be working hard to get open for the next pass. Indeed, often the person with the ball should be the only one who looks relatively passive and calm.

I am not saying that, when you have the ball, you should just stand there with it or lay down and take a nap. If you get the ball with tons of empty space in front of you, or with a good opportunity to create a quality shot on goal, then, by all means, crank up the intensity and make the most of the opportunity. But you have to break away from the idea that *every* time you get the ball, it's your turn to dribble forward until you either score a goal or lose it trying. No matter what position you play and no matter how good you are, this is exactly the wrong thing to do – wrong because it will just result in needless turnovers – *most of the time.*

What you should be doing instead, most of the time, is passing the ball quickly to an open teammate and then using your energy to get yourself open to receive the next pass in an even more advantageous position.

We can summarize this way. To score goals, your team will typically need to complete something like 10 consecutive passes. But if everybody who doesn't have the ball just stands in place, with a defender either on them or between them and the ball, the person with the ball won't have any easy passing options, and the team won't be able to maintain possession long enough to create an opportunity to score. So it is crucial that whenever somebody else on your team has the ball, you make it easy for him to see that you are a good passing option. You do this by moving into the seams between defenders and, as needed, moving toward the ball (but then also, if you don't get it, clearing out to create space for someone else and to get yourself into a position to start the cycle again).

You do it, that is, by yelling with your legs.

# CHAPTER 3

---

# We Want Width

*"...it's so simple: when you have possession you make the field big and when you lose the ball you make it small again. That's a fundamental principle that you can learn in childhood."*

- Johan Cruyff

THE last chapter was all about the need to be continuously moving into spaces where you can receive a pass. We stressed in particular the idea of moving into seams between defenders. But there is one place – or, more precisely, there are two places – where you can almost always be open without being in a gap between defenders: out wide, near the sidelines.

The reason there is space there is that the defenders are trying to prevent your team from scoring, and the goal is, horizontally speaking, in the center of the field. So the defenders will always want to drift in toward the center, to more effectively guard the area in front of the goal.

This typically leaves acres and acres of empty space out wide, and we can take advantage of that space in several ways.

First, if being wide means being wide open, then that is an inherently good place to be. Being wide open means you are a good passing option for whichever player on your team has the ball, and it means that when you get the ball you will have plenty of space and time to do something smart with it.

Second, your being wide open out wide tends to lure defenders out wide to mark or pressure you. But from our point of view as the team with the ball, a defense that is spread out is a defense that is *spread thin.* The gaps between the defenders (which our players, yelling with their legs, are constantly trying to find and exploit) get wider. And there are then fewer defenders protecting the area in the center, in front of the goal. Both of these massively improve our chances of scoring.

There is also a third (and relatively under-appreciated) way in which width is valuable. In the last chapter we talked about the need to sometimes move toward the player with the ball to get open for a pass. You need to do this when the defenders move to pinch off the passing lane, and/or when your teammate with the ball is under intense pressure, is in danger of losing the ball, and urgently needs an easy and quick outlet. But, to put it simply, you can't move toward the ball if you are already too close to it. Starting wide creates space for you to move into, back toward the middle of the field, if and when you need to.

Let's see what the value of width looks like in a few concrete situations.

# 3.1 ⚽ Wingers

Teams play with many different formations. Maybe you play 9v9 with a 3-4-1 formation (that is, one goalie, three defenders, four midfielders, and one forward). Or maybe you play 11v11 in a 4-4-2. Or a 4-3-3. Or a 3-5-2.

But whatever formation your team plays, there will be two designated players – usually called the "wings" or "wingers" (or, in certain formations, "wing-backs") – whose fundamental job is to maintain the team's width. This job is assigned to the two outside midfielders in a 3-4-1 or a 4-4-2, maybe to the two outside forwards in a 4-3-3, etc. The details will vary somewhat from team to team, formation to formation, and coach to coach. But the essence of the job is the same in any system: be a wide-open passing option when things get clogged in one part of the field and we need to switch the point of attack.

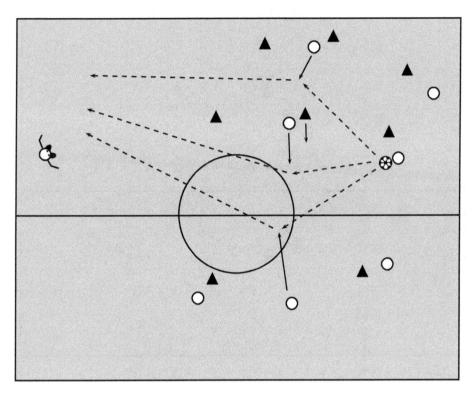

*Figure 3A: The black triangles have done a good job of clogging the path forward on the right hand side, and almost everybody on our white circles team has drifted over to that side as well. We need to switch the point of attack! And because you, the left winger, have kept your width, you are a fantastic passing option for whoever gets the ball (the center back stepping up, the other center mid dropping back, or the forward dropping back). And you'll have tons of space and time when you get it. (Note, incidentally, that of the three pictured options for getting the ball out to you on the left wing, the backwards pass to the center back is probably the best because there is the least pressure and the center back has the best perspective to see the situation. The dropping center mid might have a difficult time seeing and completing the next pass to you out on the wing, but a good center mid will make it happen. The passing sequence that goes through the forward is also a good option, but it might only be possible if the center mid yells with his legs and pulls the black triangle's center mid with him as shown.)*

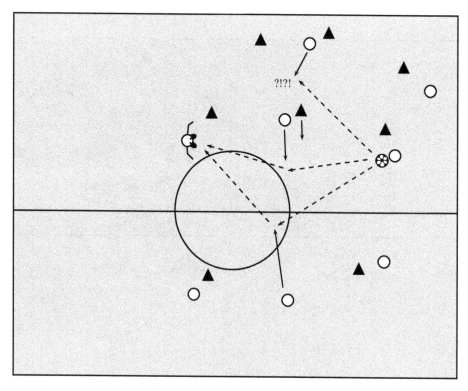

*Figure 3B: Compared to Figure 3A, the situation shown here is much, much worse because you, the left wing, have gotten sucked in toward the middle of the field. Some of the passing sequences that could have gotten you the ball if you had stayed wide, are simply no longer available. Other sequences can still happen, but get you the ball in a much worse position: you're immediately pressured and have very few options other than forcing the ball back into the clogged right-hand side.*

The typical situation is illustrated in Figure 3A. The ball has been on the right-hand side of the field for a while, so the opposing team has shifted almost completely to that side to clog the attack. Our white circles team needs to switch fields – needs to move the ball over to the left side where there is a lot of open space and maybe a path to a goal-scoring opportunity. And this is accomplished quite easily because you, the left wing, have stayed wide. Because you resisted the temptation to drift over toward the middle of the field, almost any player on your team can get you the ball by just putting it into the space in front of you. And, again, because you stayed on the left sideline even while everybody else on the field was drifting to the right, you'll still have tons of space and time (to dribble at the goal) even after you run forward to pick up the ball. It's really a glorious situation.

Now take a look at Figure 3B and note, by contrast, how poor the situation would be if, instead of staying wide, you had succumbed to temptation and drifted, with everyone else, toward the center of the field.

This is why it is so important that wingers stay near their sidelines, even when everybody else is drifting to one side of the field... *especially* when everybody else is drifting to one side of the field.

We want width!

## 3.2 ☻ Outside backs

The left and right fullbacks are another crucial source of width in virtually every formation. Of course, along with the center back(s), the outside backs are designated defenders. And as mentioned above (in the context of discussing the other team) defenders generally want and need to stay somewhat central, to protect the goal they are defending.

It is thus a common and good thing – when the other team has the ball – for the (let's say, three) defenders to arrange themselves as shown in Figure 3C. (Note that the black triangle team here does not have a lot of width and therefore allows our defenders to simultaneously guard the most threatening players and protect the central area in front of the goal.)

But suppose the other team takes an ill-advised long shot or attempts an unsuccessful through-ball, or one of our players steals the ball away and passes backwards, so that now our goalie has the ball at his feet. The new situation is shown in Figure 3D.

Suddenly, our team's lack of width is a huge problem! Any reasonably short, on-the-ground pass that the goalie could try to make would put the team into a very dangerous situation. For example, if he passes to you, the right back, you will receive the ball facing backwards and with a goal-hungry opponent right on your heels. You could try to turn with the ball and dribble past the opponent, but if you don't succeed it's an almost-certain goal for the other

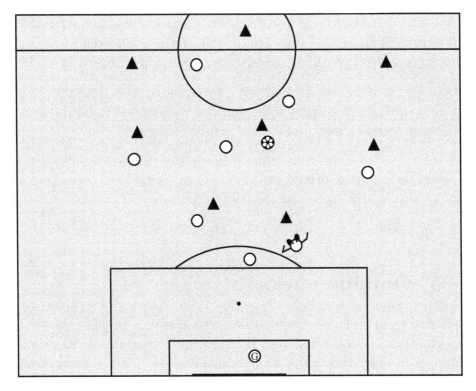

*Figure 3C: As the other team brings the ball down, the three defenders stay between the other team's attackers and our goal and try to protect the dangerous area in front of the goal. They thus do not have a lot of width, and it would be a bad thing, in this situation, if they did!*

team. You could try a quick pass to the center back, who might be able to dribble forward, but, again, if something goes wrong your team is in serious trouble. Probably your best option would be to one-touch it immediately back to the goalie (who, after all, is the most open of all the players you have any chance of passing to), which puts the team back into exactly the situation shown in Figure 3D.

Instead of passing short, the goalie could of course try to play a longer pass to one of the midfielders. But, especially with the four midfielders all bunched up near the middle of the field, these passes are also pretty dangerous. The goalie could blast a long ball (or punt) to midfield, but, well, that's just going to be a long turnover, and possession is precious.

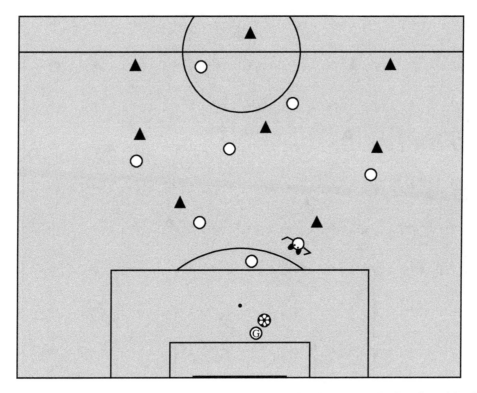

*Figure 3D: As soon as our team wins the ball, the same lack of width that made our defensive positioning strong makes our (now) offensive positioning seriously problematic.*

You can probably see what needs to happen for the team to make something positive of this situation. We want width! In particular, you and the other outside back need to create some space by spreading out wide. (And, in addition, downfield a bit, the wingers need to do the same.) The result should be something like what's shown in Figure 3E.

Now, good opportunities to pass out of the back and start developing an attack are everywhere. The two black triangle forwards simply cannot guard all three defenders when they are spread out like this. (And if they bring another person forward, that's great for us! Our goalie can simply play a longer pass to whichever midfielder is now wide open.)

Suppose the black triangles hedge their bets and keep roughly the shape shown. So the goalie takes one of several equally-good options and, let's

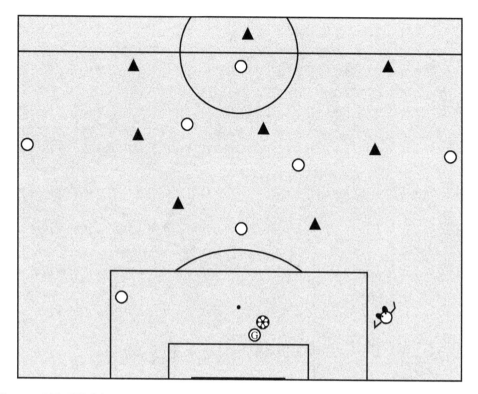

*Figure 3E: Width provides ample opportunities to build an attack out of the back.*

say, plays the ball out to you, the right back. Practically however the black triangles respond, you have excellent options.

Suppose, for example, the other team shifts hard to the right (that's our right) as shown in Figure 3F. This does clog the path forward along the right side of the field. But you know what to do in response to that. Get the ball over to the left winger, who is now wide open! (The best way to get the ball there is indicated in Figure 3F: you should just play it back to the goalie, who can pass it to the left back, who can pass it upfield to the left wing. It'll be easy to get it over there this way since a crisply passed ball moves way faster than any black triangle player can possibly run.)

OK, so what if the defense reacts differently when that initial pass from the goalie goes out to you at right back? For example, maybe the two black triangle forwards press up into the penalty area to prevent you from passing

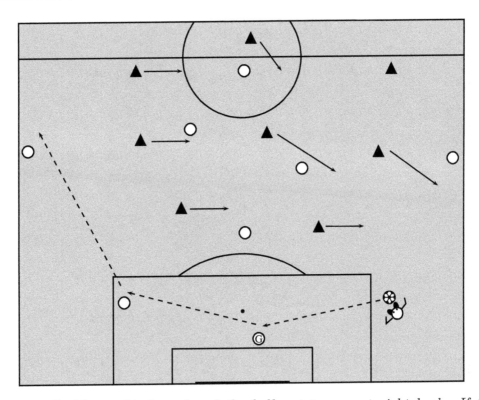

*Figure 3F: The goalie has played the ball out to you at right back. If the defense reacts by shifting to that side of the field (to prevent you from just dribbling and/or passing forward), it's no problem: you just play the ball back to the goalie, who can play it immediately out to the left back, who can play it immediately up to the left winger. (Note that the left winger better have stayed wide even when that first pass went to you at right back!)*

back toward the center, as shown in Figure 3G. Again, it's no problem. Now you're clear to just dribble forwards, passing eventually to the right winger or one of your center mids or the center back, when one of their midfielders steps up to pressure you.

Of course, there are an infinite number of slightly different ways it could play out. If one black triangle forward moves to prevent you from dribbling forward and the other moves to cut off the pass back to the goalie, then the center back will be wide open. If their two forwards split apart and mark the two outside backs, to prevent the goalie from playing the ball to one of

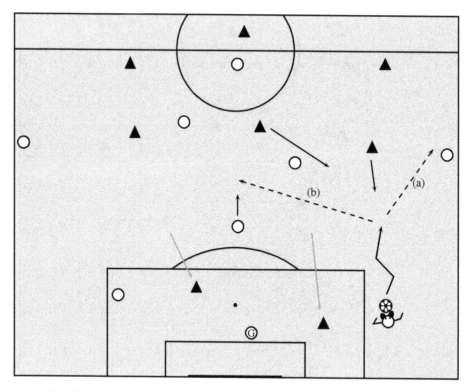

*Figure 3G: The goalie has played the ball out to you at right back. If the defense reacts by pressing hard into the penalty area (to prevent you from passing back to the goalie or center back), it's also no problem: you just dribble forward, wait for one of their midfielders to step up to pressure you, and then pass, for example, to (a) the right wing or (b) the center back. (Note that the right wing is open precisely because he stayed wide. And note that the center back has yelled with his legs, moving forward into the nice seam created when the black triangle forward moved to cut off your option of passing back to the goalie.)*

them in the first place, then again the center back will be wide open in the middle.

You see, with our goalie as part of the offensive attack we are building from the back, we have an extreme numbers advantage: it's four against two (and would be four against one if, like us, the black diamonds were playing a 3-4-1). So there are always going to be easy passing options if we are just patient, composed, and willing to take what the other team gives us.

(And in the extremely unlikely event that the black triangles get frustrated by this situation and send additional players forward, that's also no problem. In that case our goalie can just blast the ball down to midfield, knowing that this is now a smart play because we'll have a numbers advantage there.)

This happy situation is caused by the outside backs spreading wide as soon as our team wins possession of the ball. This allows us to take advantage of our superior numbers and start building an attack out of the back.

As soon as our team has possession of the ball, our outside backs should stop thinking of themselves as the last line of defense, and start thinking of themselves as the first line of offense. And, when we're on offense, we want width.

## 3.3 ⚽ Cues

It is helpful to make very explicit a point that was merely implicit in the last section. A change of possession (from "they have it" to "we have it") needs to be a *cue* for the defenders to switch from a defensive mindset ("stay central and protect the goal") to an offensive mindset ("spread out to create space and passing options"). As soon as the outside backs recognize, for example, that the goalie will establish possession of the ball (e.g., there was a shot on goal but it will be easy to save with no chance of a rebound, or someone passes the ball back to the goalie) this needs to trigger the immediate switch of mindset and the resulting movements: outside backs must literally run into the positions shown in the last few Figures.

Shots being saved by, and passes backwards to, the goalie, are two of the clearest such cues. But there are others. And the cues apply not just to the outside backs, but to the wingers and players in other positions as well. If our team wins the ball further upfield, for example, that is a similar cue for especially the outside backs and the wingers to spread out and make the field big.

Here is another example. As we discussed in the first Chapter, backwards passes are good because they are usually very low-risk ways to maintain possession of the ball. They tend to be low-risk because the player being passed to is usually wide open, so he has lots of time and space to look around and select the best available next pass.

This pause associated with a backwards pass makes it a perfect cue for everybody else on the team to reflect on their individual positioning and the overall team shape. Sometimes, for example, despite the inspired propaganda of the previous section, the wingers will get sucked in toward the middle of the field during the heat of play. For example, maybe the other team had the ball for a while and they had to pinch in to help out defensively. Or maybe they moved toward the ball to provide a hotly-pressured teammate an emergency passing option. It happens! The point is, a backwards pass, anywhere on the field, provides a breath-catching moment for the team as a whole. Wingers should use it as a cue to remember their primary job and reposition themselves as needed.

Temporary stoppages of play – such as throw-ins and goal-kicks, and free kicks resulting from foul calls – are also cues for outside backs and wingers to evaluate (and, if needed, correct) their positioning.

Just remember, when we have the ball, we want width!

## 3.4  ⚽  Stay in your lane

So far, we have mostly focused on the importance of width for midfielders and defenders. But width can be of vital importance for attackers as well.

Let me start by sharing something I saw just a couple weeks ago in one of my kids' indoor games. (It is important for the example that in our indoor league, there is no offsides.) One player on our team stole the ball from one of the opponent's defenders, near midfield. The opponent's other defender had pushed forward, and so was now out of position. But our other forward had remained near midfield, so we had a classic 2-on-1 fast-break opportunity.

Unfortunately, our other forward – the one without the ball – did what turns out to be the worst possible thing in that situation: he ran to the penalty spot, right in front of our player who was dribbling with the ball. See Figure 3H for an illustration.

I think I know what our player was thinking. He recognized that we had a

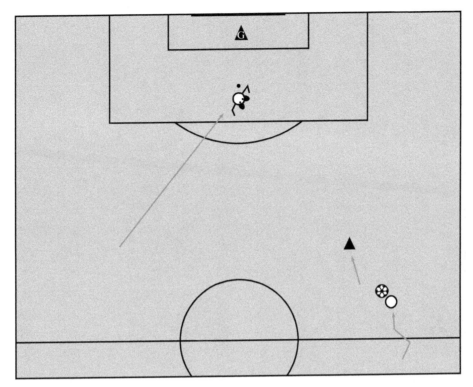

*Figure 3H: In a recent indoor game, we had a great 2-v-1 fast break oppor-*
*tunity, but the player without the ball – let's call him "you" – spoiled it by*
*running as shown here. (Note that, in the indoor league, there is no offside*
*rule. So the problem with the run shown here is not that it puts you in an*
*offside position. Instead, the problem is that it makes it possible for the lone*
*black triangle defender to simultaneously prevent your teammate's two best*
*options: dribbling toward the goal and passing to you.)*

good attacking opportunity, and ran to the most aggressively attacky place
he could think of, i.e., the place where he would most like to receive a pass,
should the player with the ball be able to deliver one to him.

Of course, the problem is that he went to basically the one place on the field
where it was impossible for the player with the ball to actually make that
delivery!

The point could be put this way: our player did not do a good job of seeking the seams. When there is only one defender in the picture, practically

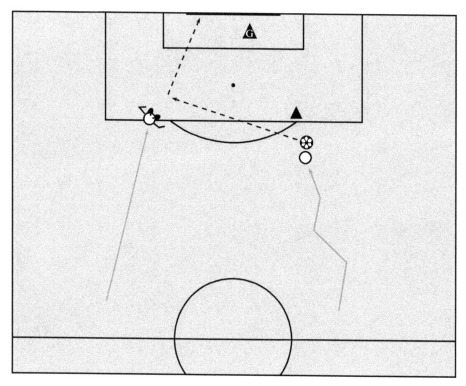

*Figure 3I: Maintain width on a 2-v-1 fast break to put the defender in an impossible situation!*

everywhere on the entire field is along a seam... everywhere, that is, except the line behind the defender from where the ball is.

It is helpful to think of it from the defender's point of view as well. What makes a 2-v-1 fast break such a good opportunity for the offense, and such a nightmare for the lone defender, is that the offense has two options: either the player with the ball can dribble up and score, or he can dish the ball off to his teammate who can score. The problem, for the defender, is that he cannot prevent both options. If he pressures the ball, the guy with the ball will pass it to his open teammate. And if he blocks the pass, the guy with the ball will just dribble.

From that point of view, the problem with the run shown in Figure 3H was that he put himself in one of the very few positions that would allow the lone defender to simultaneously defend both options: he could pressure the ball and stop the dribbler from dribbling forward *and*, simultaneously, block the pass.

As it turned out, the defender did just that, and we failed to score.

So what should our player have done differently? What would you do in that situation? If you're thinking "we want width!" you are exactly right.

We want to force the defender to make an impossible choice: do I stay between the ball and the goal (so the guy with the ball can't shoot, but then the pass is wide open), or do I step between the ball and the open teammate (so the guy with the ball can't pass, but then the shot is wide open)?

To put the defender in that impossible situation, our players just need to move forward with the ball while maintaining width, so that the two players and the goal form a triangle instead of a straight line. See Figure 3I for one of the two ways this fast break opportunity might have had a happier ending.

## 3.5 ⚽ Attack the gap

As one final example, let's see how width can create a devastating attack out of a situation that may not seem like much of a fast-break opportunity at all.

Suppose, as shown in Figure 3J, we have the ball, near midfield, with three attacking players. The black triangles have three defenders back, each near one of our players. So the black triangles have decent pressure on the ball and everyone else is marked up. It doesn't seem like a great opportunity for us.

But because our three players are spread wide, the gaps between the defenders are very large. So, for example, when the initial pass goes to the player on the right (who moves toward the ball to make sure he gets to it first), the defenders will tend to react as shown. In particular, the defender in the middle will move to the right, partly just with the natural tendency to follow the motion of the ball, and partly to try to prevent a defense-splitting pass between him and the defender on the right. But the gap was so big to start with that this small adjustment is nowhere near enough to close it. So our right winger can play the one-touch penetrating pass in behind the defense,

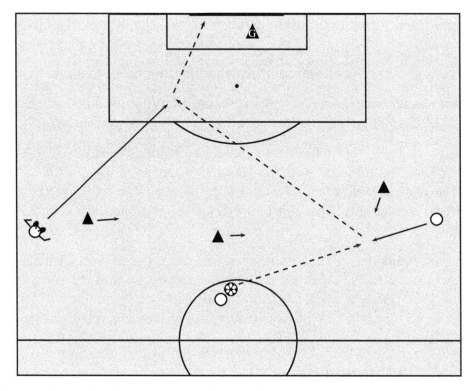

*Figure 3J: A simple example of how width can generate large gaps between defenders which quick passing and effective movement can exploit to create goals.*

and our left winger can run onto it and put the ball into the back of the net.

You might think that the black triangle's right back (the one on our left, marking our left wing) would track back with our left wing and be in a position to intercept the penetrating pass. If he is a truly excellent defender, he might have a chance of doing that.

But think about what happens from his point of view. Initially, when everybody is in the positions shown in Figure 3J, he is probably facing toward the bottom of the Figure, so that he can simultaneously see (to his right) the guy he is marking (our left wing) and also (to his left) the ball. But when the ball is played to our right winger, this defender will naturally turn a little bit further to his left (and probably also begin moving that way, as indicated) so he can see what happens with the ball. He will therefore simply not be able to see that, moments later, our left wing makes the jump to hyperspace, sprinting in behind him to receive the pass and score. More likely, he'll continue turning to his left wondering "Who in the world is that next pass going to?" only to realize, far too late, that it's going to the guy he thought he was still marking.

Attacking with width spreads the defense thin and makes it harder for individual defenders to simultaneously see everything they'd like to be able to keep an eye on. This makes it easier for us to score goals!

## 3.6 ⚽ Overview

When our team has the ball, we want to pass the ball around, maintain possession, and eventually create an opportunity to score a goal by exploiting a gap between defenders or an area where there are no defenders. All parts of this plan are made easier if our team takes full advantage of all of the available space. When we spread out wide, instead of bunching up in the middle of the field, our wide players are more open for passes and have more time and space on the ball when they get it. Plus, when we are spread out, the defense has to spread out to cover us, which creates bigger seams and gaps in the middle. So there's no doubt about it. We want width!

# CHAPTER 4

---

# Discover Depth

*"Take rugby. The players have to pass the ball backward to be able to run forward. As a result, they have a better overview of what's happening in front of them. The same theory can be applied to football [i.e., soccer], but a lot of people don't see it that way. They think they have to play the ball forward, when in fact the man coming up the field from behind is the one they should be playing to. He's in a deeper position, but he has an overview."*

- Johan Cruyff

THE last Chapter was all about the value of width – i.e., of good horizontal spacing of players across the field. But how players position themselves *vertically* – up and down or forward and backward along the field – is also crucially important. Good vertical positioning is what we mean by "depth" and will be discussing in this Chapter.

To some extent, proper vertical spacing is obvious and is, indeed, inherent in the names we give to different positions: forwards should be forward, midfielders should be in the middle, and backs should be back. Duh. But we can and will dig more deeply into, for example, how the backs should position themselves, vertically, relative to one another, and similarly for other positions.

We have already seen at least two very clear examples of the value of depth. Way back in Chapter 1, we talked about the value of passing backwards to the goalkeeper when you have the ball as the outside back and the way forward is clogged, as in Figure 1A, or when you arrive first at the other team's attempted long-ball and have opponents nipping at your heels, as in Figure 1C. In both of these situations, the pass to the goalie is a fantastic option because you can see that she is wide open. So passing to her is *safe* and she has a lot of time and space to figure out the smartest thing to do with the ball after she gets it. All of this is made possible by the goalie's *depth*.

Let's examine the importance and value of depth in some other situations.

## 4.1  ⚽  Center backs

Consider the situation illustrated in Figure 4A. Our right back (in a 3-4-1 formation) has the ball. The black triangle team's left forward is stepping up to apply pressure along a line that effectively prevents our right back from passing out to our right wing. (More on that soon!) Neither of our center mids has managed to find a seam through which the right back feels comfortable passing them the ball.

In the situation pictured, the right back's best option is probably to play the ball all the way back to the goalie. Of course, the goalie is a *long* way behind the ball. That's OK, although one point about vertical spacing that could be made is that the goalie should probably move forward, say, to the top of the penalty area. Then, if the right back does play the ball backwards to her, we don't give up quite as much yardage and the keeper can swing the ball across to the left back, say, that much quicker.

But let's go back to the situation pictured in Figure 4A and think about what you, the center back, are doing. You really should be providing the right back with a viable passing option. As you have positioned yourself, though, a pass to you is incredibly dangerous. Because you are even with – i.e., at the same vertical level as – the right back, there are no other defenders behind either of you. So if the right back tries to pass to you and the black triangle forward intercepts it, she'll be able to dribble unimpeded at the goal and probably score.

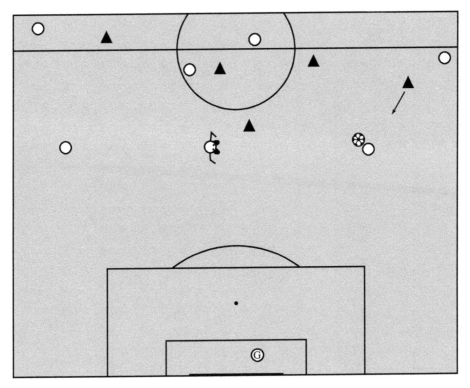

*Figure 4A: Our right back has the ball with black triangle pressure closing in. You, the center back, should be providing a good passing option for her, but, at present, you are not! Where should you move and why?*

And there is an additional problem as well. You are perfectly level not only with the right back, but also with the left back. The three defenders, that is, are positioned along a perfectly horizontal straight line. Do you see why that is bad? That's right – it's bad because you (together with the black triangle forward who is marking you) are *blocking* another passing option that could otherwise have been viable, namely, a pass from the right back directly across the field to the left back.

OK, so your positioning as shown in Figure 4A is far from ideal. Where should you move instead?

Take a minute to think about that and then you can read on to see if we have the same idea in mind.

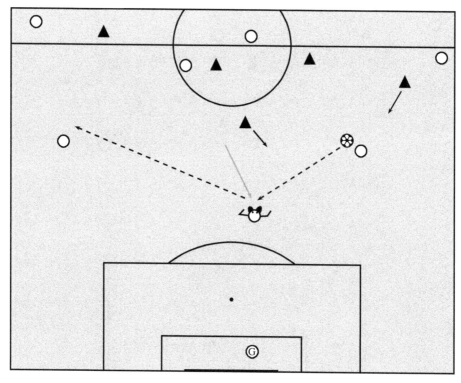

*Figure 4B: If you, the center back, simply drop backwards a little bit, relative to your position in Figure 4A, all kinds of good possibilities open up.*

My answer is that you, the center back, should simply drop backwards about 10 yards, to the position indicated in Figure 4B. You are now likely to be wide open for a diagonal backwards pass. This pass is much safer than the flat horizontal passing option you were giving the right back in your previous position: it is less likely to be intercepted, and in the (now extremely unlikely) event that the black triangle forward does somehow manage to intercept the pass, you will be in a good defensive position, between her and the goal, when she does.

But, again, in all likelihood the pass gets to you without any trouble, and you have plenty of time to make another easy pass over to the wide-open left back, as shown. Note, incidentally, that the end result here is not so different from what would probably have happened if you had stayed in your original position and the right back had played the ball back to the goalie. But it really is better for this two-pass sequence to go through you, the center back.

Why?

First, as already mentioned, it is helpful for you to be somewhat deeper than the two outside backs, just in case something goes wrong and the black triangles win the ball.

Second, the roughly 20-30 yard passes (from the right back to you, and then from you over to the left back) are, all other things being equal, more likely to be made accurately than the 40-50 yard passes that would be required to get the ball over to the left back via the goalie. (Think about what might happen, for example, if you stay in a flat line with the two outside backs, and either the pass from the right back to the goalie, or the pass from the goalie to the left back, gets mis-hit and, say, only gets halfway to its intended target.)

Third, the shorter passes (from the right back to you and then from you to the left back) are going to be completed *faster*, because they are shorter. We want to get the ball over to the left back because she is wide open, and, all other things being equal, the faster we get it to her, the more time she'll have to go forward, after she gets it, before pressure arrives.

And, believe it or not, there is an additional *fourth* advantage to dropping into the position shown in Figure 4B. This has to do with the possibility that the black triangle forward sticks with you, the center back, as you drop. As you can see in Figure 4C, this opens up a direct pass, across the field, to the left back. This pass is, admittedly, somewhat dangerous because it is so long and so flat. But it is the best available option in the situation shown. (The left back can mitigate the danger to some extent by moving toward the ball, as shown. And in the event that the long pass is mis-hit or mis-handled or intercepted, it will again turn out to be a good thing that you, the center back, dropped into a good position from which to mount an emergency defense.)

All of this illustrates a couple of important principles that are worth making explicit. First, diagonal backwards passes are much safer and better than horizontal ("flat" or "square") passes, especially on the defensive end. So, whenever possible, you should provide support *with depth* to your teammate who has the ball. Second, whenever three players are (or could be) involved

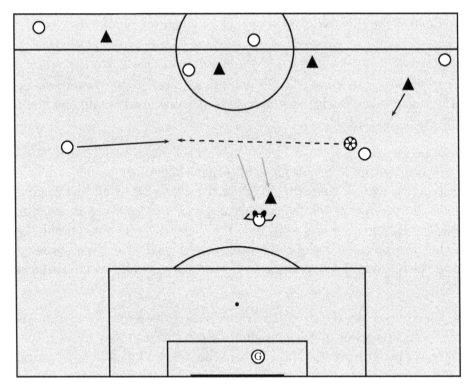

*Figure 4C: If the black triangle forward sticks with you, the center back, as you drop back to provide depth, this opens up a large gap through which the right back can pass directly to the left back (who should probably move toward the ball, as indicated, to make sure she gets to the ball first).*

in a passing sequence, triangles are good and straight lines are bad. Any time you find yourself directly between one teammate who has the ball and another teammate who could be a passing option, get the heck out of the way! Make a triangle, by dropping back or pushing forward, instead of a straight line, and you will make it impossible for any one individual player from the opposing team to simultaneously prevent both possible passes.

## 4.2 ⚽ Wingers

Let's go back to the very beginning of the scenario discussed in the last section. Recall that the right back was forced to stop going forward, and

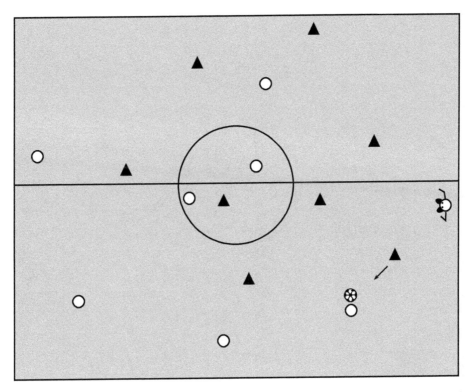

*Figure 4D: The black triangle left wing is pressuring our right back, with the ball, as shown. If you are the right wing, how could you move to give the right back a good passing option?*

start considering a backwards pass to the goalie or center back, because the center mids weren't getting open and, in particular, because the black triangle's left mid was doing a nice job of simultaneously pressuring the ball and cutting off the pass to our right winger.

Suppose you are our right winger in this situation, which I have reproduced (with you in your new starring role) in Figure 4D. What could you be doing instead of just standing there, watching the show, as your teammate with the ball is forced to slow down, stop, turn around, and move the ball backwards? If your answer was "Jump up and down in place, wave my arms around, and yell for the ball, even though my teammate couldn't possibly pass to me because there's an opponent between the ball and me" you should probably go back and re-read Chapter 2. But of course you didn't say that!

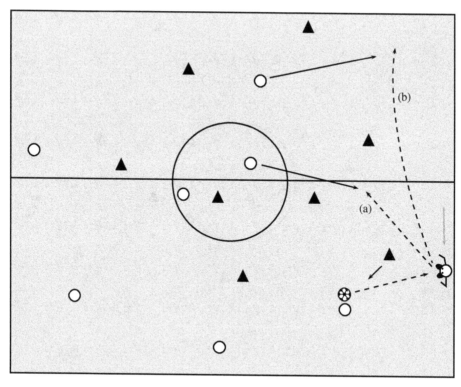

*Figure 4E: By moving backwards along the sideline, i.e., by adjusting your depth, you give your teammate a good passing option and create a number of good subsequent attacking opportunities.*

Instead, I know you said that you should "yell with your legs," i.e., move yourself into a place where your teammate can easily pass the ball to your feet. One possibility would be to move horizontally (toward the middle of the field) into the gap between the black triangle midfielders. But this would leave you with the ball in a pretty mediocre situation: you'd be facing backwards and would be surrounded by opposing players.

So, especially having read Chapter 3 and hence recognizing the value of keeping your width, you decide to stay along the sideline and instead show for the ball by changing your *depth*. The way to do this, and two possible nice passes you might make next, are shown in Figure 4E: (a) you could lay the ball off to your center midfielder, who does a nice job of seeking the seam between the two black triangles and moving toward the ball, or (b) you could

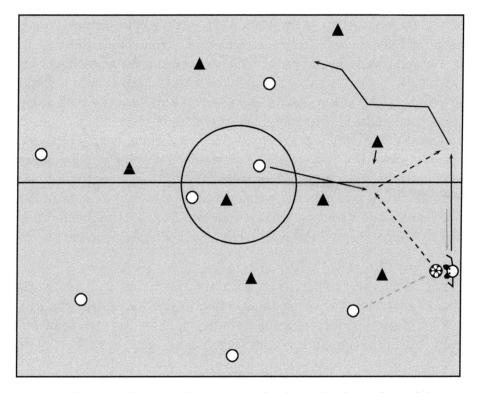

*Figure 4F: If, immediately after moving backwards along the sideline to receive the ball from the right back, you play it to your center mid, you can now reverse direction, sprint forward along the sideline, and get the ball back from the center mid with room to dribble in toward the goal.*

play a longer forward pass into a space along the sideline where your team's striker can go collect it.

Both of these options are created because you adjusted your depth to make sure you were a viable passing option.

Incidentally, I can't help pointing out what could happen next if you make pass (a) from Figure 4E. Having moved backwards along the sideline to get open for the pass from the right back and having played the quick ball into the center midfielder, you are now in a great position to immediately change direction and go *forward* along the sideline to receive a quick return pass from your center midfielder. This sequence is shown in Figure 4F.

You might be wondering: why wouldn't I just dribble forward along the sideline after I get the ball from the right back? You could, and that would not be the worst thing in the world. But you can run faster without the ball than with it, so if the give-and-go sequence with the center mid is available, that is definitely the better option. You will end up with the ball, along the sideline beyond midfield, *faster* and will therefore be more likely to be able to get in behind the black triangle defender who is lurking nearby. Playing the give-and-go, instead of just dribbling forward, also helps you get past that opposing player in a second way: she will naturally step forward, as indicated in Figure 4F, when you play the pass into the center mid in front of her. So she'll be leaning the wrong way to prevent you from getting behind her and zig-zagging your way with the ball toward the goal, after you get the return pass.

The point of all this is that, even with the restriction that, as a winger, you should generally stay along the sideline to provide width, you can still create a lot of good opportunities, for yourself and for your team, by moving vertically – by adjusting and re-adjusting your *depth*.

The example also provides another important illustration of the idea, mentioned in the last section, that diagonal passes are generally preferable to square passes. In the last section, we talked about how square passes, between defenders, are dangerous because, if they are intercepted, neither the passer nor the intended recepient is in a good position to defend. It is therefore safer to pass backwards along a diagonal.

Forward-diagonal passes are also preferable to square passes for the same reason: if the pass is intercepted, the passer is in a good position to defend. But they are preferable for another reason as well: assuming the pass is completed as intended, a forward-diagonal pass makes it impossible for the opposing player, who was pressuring the passer, to now pressure the new ball-holder by simply shifting over.

To see this, go back and look at Figure 4E but imagine that you, the winger, moved backwards along the sideline just a few yards further, so that the pass from the right back to you is horizontal instead of diagonal. See how, by just shifting to the right (i.e., to her left) the black triangle forward could then pressure you, perhaps winning the ball or at least cutting off the passing options shown in that Figure?

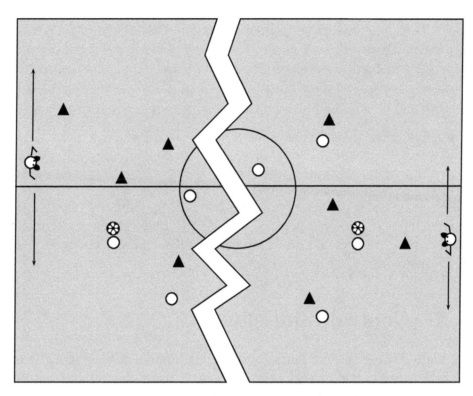

*Figure 4G: Two independent scenarios are shown in this one Figure to save space. In the scenario on the left, our left back has the ball and you are the left wing. In the scenario on the right, one of the central midfielders has the ball and you are the right wing. In both scenarios, you have to decide where to move. Should you go forward, or backward?*

*Here's what I think. In the scenario on the right, you could get open for a nice forward-diagonal pass by pushing forward, or you could get open for a nice backward-diagonal pass by dropping back. All other things being equal, we'd rather go forward than backward, so you should go forward. Just make sure you don't go too far, before the ball is played to you, or you might be offsides! The scenario on the left is a little trickier. If you push forward, you make yourself less open, not more open. You could get open for a backwards-diagonal pass by dropping back along the sidelines, but without much pressure on the ball it doesn't seem like we need to go backwards. If I were the left winger in this situation, I would just stay where I am. I am technically open for a forward-diagonal pass right where I'm standing. Why mess with a good thing?*

Similarly, look again at Figure 4F, but imagine that the return pass, from the center mid back out to you on the wing, was horizontal, parallel to the midfield line, instead of forward-diagonal. In that case, the nearby black diamond player would have a much better chance of just stepping to her left and blocking your way forward.

The principle that this illustrates is that, as a winger, you want to move vertically, along the sideline, so that you are, at all times, open for the most aggressive possible diagonal pass.

I invite you to test out your own understanding by thinking about the two (independent) scenarios pictured in Figure 4G. In each case, where should the winger position herself, and why? After you've thought about it, you can read my answers in the Figure's caption.

## 4.3  ⚽  Central midfielders

We have already encountered most of the crucial points about vertical spacing in our discussions of center backs and wingers. The application of these points to the positioning of midfield players is extremely important. But I think once you understand the points, it is easy to see how and why they apply in the middle of the field, so we can be a little more brief.

To begin with, formations with two (or even sometimes three) central midfielders are extremely common. Probably more than players in any other position, central midfielders need to be constantly working to adjust and readjust their position, seeking seams and moving toward the ball as needed, to provide passing options to their teammates. But because there are two (or even three) of them, it is crucial that they work together, responding not only to how the ball, their other teammates, and the opponents are moving, but also to how their fellow center mids are moving.

For example, consider the situation shown in Figure 4H. You are one of the two center midfielders in a 3-4-1. The right winger has the ball and is being pressured from both the front and the back, so she desperately needs a passing option in the middle of the field. Unfortunately, you and the other center mid are perfectly level with the ball (in a straight line), so the black triangle's center mid is blocking potential passes to both of you. The other

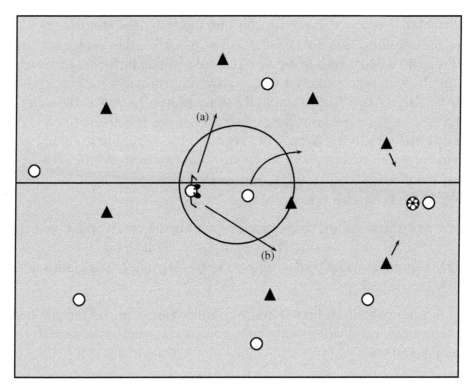

*Figure 4H: The right wing has the ball and needs passing options towards the middle of the field. The other center mid moves forward, into a seam between two black triangles. You could (a) move forward into that same seam, but deeper, looking for a pass from the other center mid after she gets the ball from the winger. Or you could (b) move backwards into a different seam to provide a second passing option for the winger. What do you think is the better option?*

center mid hops into action, yelling with her legs and moving forward, into one of the seams, as shown.

This leaves you with (at least) two options. You could (a) also run forward, with the hope that if the pass goes in to the other center mid, she can turn and pass to you, and you can perhaps create a 2-v-1 against the black triangle's center back with your team's striker. Or (b) you could show for a backwards-diagonal pass in the other seam.

Which option do you think is better here?

In my opinion, option (a) is not terrible and might indeed create a good goal-scoring opportunity. But note that it leaves you, the other center midfielder, and the right winger with the ball, in a now tilted but still very straight line. So the two center mids, together, are only providing a single passing option to the player with the ball. That's admittedly better than the zero passing options you were providing a second before. But if the black triangle center mid has eyes in the back of her head (and you shouldn't laugh, because all good center mids *do*), she'll know that she can prevent the pass by just shifting her position a little bit. And in that case, your team is in serious trouble if you went with option (a).

That's why I think option (b) is much better. If the other center mid moves to provide a forward-diagonal passing option to the player with the ball, you move to provide an alternative, backward-diagonal passing option to the player with the ball.

Converting straight lines into triangles creates more and better passing options and makes good things happen – not just on the defensive end, but in the midfield as well.

## 4.4 ⚽ Passing backwards to score

Let's finally consider a way that appropriate depth – and in particular a backwards-diagonal pass – can create a beautiful goal-scoring opportunity.

The scenario pictured in Figure 4I happens all of the time in soccer: a winger gets the ball with space out on the sideline, manages to get around the other team's outside back, and is thus dribbling toward the goal along the end-line. Panic and mayhem erupt in front of the goal! The black diamond goalie races to the near post and the black diamond defenders madly try to pressure the ball and mark up our forward, who is also moving toward the ball to try to get open for an easy tap-in goal.

Sometimes in this situation the right winger will try to shoot, but this rarely works for reasons of simple geometry. From this angle, the target is just not very big and the goalie has it pretty well blocked off.

Sometimes the winger will try to pass the ball in to the forward for that easy tap-in goal. This does sometimes work, but usually there is so much mayhem

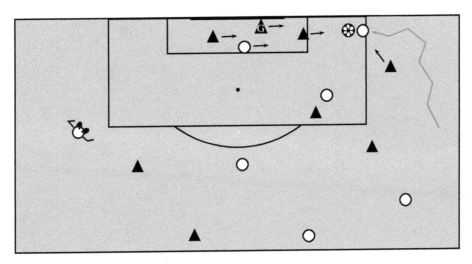

*Figure 4I: Our right winger has gotten around the black triangle team's left back in the corner and is dribbling, along the end line, toward the goal.*

in front of the goal that either the ball never quite gets to the forward (e.g., it is blocked en route by the black triangle's center back) or it gets there but the forward is getting mauled from behind just as the ball arrives and she can't cleanly deflect the ball into the goal.

(Another thing that sometimes happens is that the winger never really decides whether to shoot or pass, so she does both/neither – a "shass". This tends to work about as well as you'd guess from the way that word sounds.)

But here is another promising possibility that, in my opinion, teams implement too rarely. Instead of jamming the ball into the mayhem in front of the goal, the winger can take advantage of the fact that (almost) everybody is right in front of the goal (because almost everybody *expects* her to jam the ball into the mayhem in front of the goal), and just lay the ball back, diagonally and on the ground, toward the wide-open space near the penalty spot. You, our *left* winger, have been doing your wingerly duty and lurking out wide. Everybody has forgotten about you: out of sight, out of mind. But now is the perfect opportunity for you to take advantage of the space you helped create by staying wide, and run into that space, blasting the ball into the wide-open left side of the goal, as shown in Figure 4J.

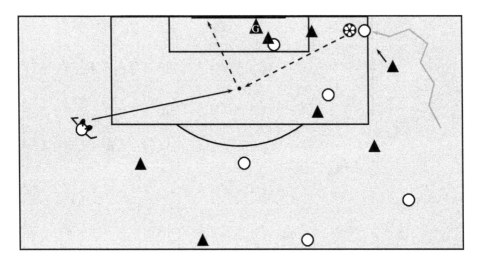

*Figure 4J: If the right winger plays a backwards-diagonal pass toward the wide-open area near the penalty spot, you, the left winger, can arrive there just at the right time to put the ball confidently into the wide-open left side of the goal. Remember, wings are only supposed to stay on the sideline until/unless there's some really good reason not to, and this definitely counts. Nice shot!*

## 4.5 ⚽ Overview

Good horizontal spacing creates space for your team to move forward. Good vertical spacing creates safer and more advantageous (typically diagonal) passing options that help your team maintain possession, move past defenders, and score goals. Reaping the rewards of good vertical positioning is easy: just discover depth!

# CHAPTER 5

---

# Face The Space

*"Baseball allowed me to focus on a lot of details that would later be very useful to me in football. As a catcher you determine the pitcher's throw because he doesn't have an overview of the whole field and you do. I learned that you had to know where you were going to throw the ball before you received it, which meant that you had to have an idea of all the space around you and where each player was before you made your throw. No football coach ever told me that I had to know where I was going to pass the ball before I had received it, but later on when I was playing football professionally the lessons from baseball – to focus on having a total overview – came back to me, and became my strength."*

- Johan Cruyff

THE last two Chapters focused on the horizontal and vertical aspects of positioning – where you should be, in different situations, to open up safer and more abundant passing options that help your team possess the ball, get forward, and score goals. But even if you are in exactly the right position, in a given situation, there is an additional factor that is of absolutely crucial importance to your ability to receive a pass and do the smartest possible thing with the ball afterwards. This factor is: which way your body is pointing, i.e., which way you are facing.

Let's start by discussing why this matters.

# 5.1 ☺ The value of vision

Recall the situation shown, for example, in Figure 4B. Our right back has the ball. Neither center mid is open, and the right wing is not moving vertically the way she should to provide a passing option out wide. The good news for the team is that you, the center back, have dropped back nicely to provide some depth, so the right back smartly makes a backwards-diagonal pass to you.

The question is: which way should you be facing as the ball comes? Take a look at Figure 5A. The upper panel and lower panel show precisely the same situation, except for one difference: in the upper panel you are facing directly toward the incoming ball, whereas in the bottom panel you are facing directly forward so that the ball is coming from your right. Which orientation is better, and why?

Take a minute to study the Figure and think about which way it would be better to be facing. And try to articulate exactly what the advantages are of facing the better way.

Once you have a clear idea in mind of what's better, and why, read on to see if we are thinking about it the same way.

So, one thing that might be considered good about the orientation in the top frame (where you're facing directly at the incoming ball) is that it focuses your attention on the incoming ball and gives you some flexibility about how to control it when it arrives: if the pass comes in a little too far forward, you can reach out and control it with your left foot, whereas if it comes in a little too far back, you can reach out and control it with your right foot.

But there are some serious problems with your orientation in that top frame as well. In particular, there are two really important things that you might not even be aware of if you are facing that way.

One is the fact that your left fullback is wide open, and you should almost certainly pass the ball over to her after you get it. But how will you pass to her if she's behind you, so you don't even know she's over there, wide open? The simple answer is: you won't.

The other crucially important thing that's happening is that the other team's

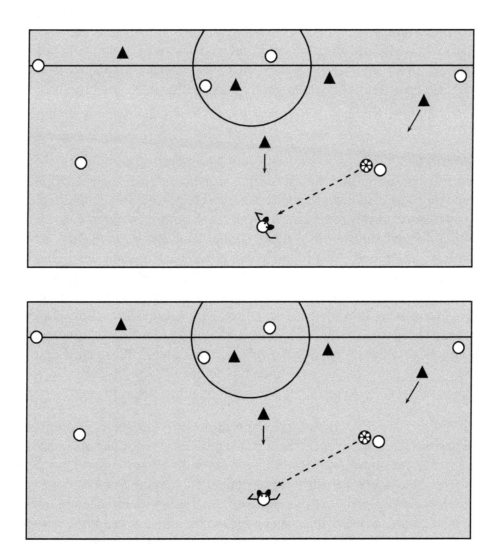

*Figure 5A: The right fullback passes the ball backwards-diagonally to you, the center back, in the situation shown. In the upper panel, you are facing directly toward the incoming ball, whereas in the lower panel you are facing forward so that the ball is coming in from your right. Which orientation is better and why?*

forward is barreling down on you. If you are facing the incoming ball, as in the top frame of Figure 5A, you might not even notice this. At best, it will be on the periphery of your awareness (because you can only see her with your peripheral vision). But this could prove disastrous! If you trap the ball, planning to then turn with it to your left to see whether maybe the left back is open for a pass, that black triangle forward could easily steal the ball away from you, take a couple of quick touches forward, and score a goal, before you even know what hit you.

I said something in the last chapter about how good center midfielders have eyes in the backs of their heads. That was not a joke, and it applies to everyone, not just center midfielders. As a soccer player, you should regularly turn your head quickly, checking over your shoulder, so you know what's happening not only in front of you but behind you. Having said that, though, the truth is that nobody *literally* has eyes in the back of their head, and even the players who do the very best possible job of regularly checking over their shoulders, will still always have a much better awareness of what's in front of them, than what's behind them. And, let's be honest, many players (I don't want to say "probably including you", but...) do not do "the very best possible job of regularly checking over their shoulders." That is, the normal situation, even for good players, is to be *significantly* more aware of what's happening in front of them, than what's happening behind them.

This is the fundamental reason why the direction you face is so important. There are certain spaces on the field where crucially relevant things are happening. Your teammates are getting open (or failing to get open!) for passes, opponents are running at you to apply pressure, moving to close down passing lanes, etc. You want to give yourself the best possible chance of being aware of as many of these things as possible. So you have to know, in a given situation, what those most important areas are, and literally point your body toward them so you can see what's going on. You have to face the space.

For you as the center back in the example situation of Figure 5A, the crucial space is basically the area in front of you (including both sides), i.e., the entire area that is shown in the Figure. (Unless you stole your goalie's lunch money at school yesterday or something, you hopefully don't need to worry too much about what's happening behind you.) This is why, as the center back in this situation, you should – without even a shred of doubt – be facing forward, as in the lower panel of Figure 5A. Facing the ball, as in the upper frame of that Figure, is simply wrong.

The same principle applies no matter what position you are playing. Its application is relatively straightforward for goalies (for whom it is basically identical to what we've just said for center backs) and also for outside backs and wingers (who generally just need to face the center of the field). So instead of talking about those cases in detail, I will trust you to look back through some of the Figures from earlier Chapters, where I have tried to be careful to always show players receiving the ball facing in the correct direction.

We'll talk more about central midfielders and forwards, for whom the question of what direction to face is a little more complicated, in later sections.

But seriously, right now, flip back and take a look at the direction the right back is facing when she receives the ball in Figure 1A. Is there anything important going on that would be relevant to deciding what to do with the ball, that she doesn't know about because she can't see it? Nope! She's able to see everything that's happening and hence weigh, in the moment, all the options we considered for her.

Now look back again at the way the left wing is facing, as the ball comes to him (by one of several possible routes) in Figure 3A. He can see literally everything happening on the entire field (with the possible exception of his goalie 80 yards back – an acceptable omission given his position on the field and the direction he's going to go with the ball when it arrives).

Look again at the way the goal-scoring forward is facing as the ball comes to him in Figure 3I. He can see his teammate, the defender, the goalie, and the target he's shooting at.

Look at the way the right wing is facing as the ball comes to her in Figure 4E. By keeping her back to the sideline she can see literally the entire field. And note in particular that she's facing that way even though she just ran backwards along the sideline to get open for the pass. This is an important point. When you are running, you usually need to be facing the way you're going. But as you arrive at the place where you're going to receive the pass, you should not just continue facing whatever direction you happened to have been running to get there. You should, if needed, turn and face the space as you receive the ball.

And, finally, look at the way the left wing is facing as she runs toward the penalty spot for the glorious finish in Figure 4J.

No, seriously, actually flip back and look again at these Figures to appreciate how valuable it is to be facing the correct direction.

It's cool, I'll wait.

## 5.2 ⊙ Receive with the back foot

The discussion in the last section was all about what you can see. Basically, you want to be facing the direction that allows you to see all (or as many as possible) of the things that might be relevant to deciding what to do with the ball when it comes. More available information means better, smarter decisions.

But there is another reason the direction you are facing is important.

Consider again the situation shown in Figure 5A. And suppose in particular that you are facing the incoming ball, as shown in the top frame of the Figure. We talked before about how, facing this way, you probably won't even be aware that your left back is wide open behind you, and so you won't even be able to consider the possibility of passing it to her.

But suppose you *were* aware of her – say, because you checked over your left shoulder just as the ball was played to you. It is *still* seriously problematic to be facing the incoming ball, as in the top frame of the Figure. Even knowing that she's wide open over there, how are you going to pass the ball to her when you're facing the other way?

The answer is: slowly, at best.

Here's what I mean. It's not that it's impossible to pass the ball to somebody 30 yards behind you. It's just impossible to do quickly, because you have to take a couple of touches on the ball to get it over to the other side of your body, and rotate your body, so that you're facing the target with the ball in front of you. Then you can make the pass. But doing that takes time. Not hours or minutes, but maybe a second or two. Which might not sound

*Figure 5B: Receiving with the back foot means letting the ball go across the front of your body and then trapping it with the foot that is further from where the ball came from. So if the ball is coming from your right, your first settling touch should be with the inside of your left foot, as shown here. (If, instead, the ball had been coming from your left side, you would want to let it roll across the front of your body and then trap it with the inside of your right foot.) Receiving the ball in this way leaves the ball directly in front of the center of your body, so you can play it in either direction – to the right with the inside of your left foot, or to the left with the inside of your right foot, or straight forward with either foot – with your very next touch. Receive the ball this way, and you can settle it and then play a crisp pass in literally any direction you can see, with the minimum number of touches and hence the minimum delay.*

like much. But remember that the black triangle forward is running at top speed directly at you from about 10 yards away, and if she steals the ball off your feet, your team probably goes down a goal. And how long do you think it takes to run 10 yards at full speed? That's right – less than a couple of seconds!

So if you're going to complete that pass over to the wide-open left back, you're going to have to control the ball and then send it on its way *quickly*.

Happily, there is a way of controlling the ball that generally allows you to play it, quickly, in any direction you can see. You just "receive it with the back foot." What that means is shown, close-up, in Figure 5B. You let the ball go across the front of your body and control it with the inside of your "back foot," i.e., the foot that is farther from where the ball came from. So, for example, if the ball is coming from your *right* side, as shown in the Figure, then your first settling touch would be with the inside of your *left* foot. If, instead, the ball is coming from your left side, then you would want to trap the ball with the inside of your right foot. What if neither of your feet is farther from where the ball came from? The point is, this only happens if you're facing directly at – or, I suppose, directly away from – the passer. But in most situations that means you've already messed up. Turn your body and face the space!

Receiving the ball with your back foot, while facing the space, puts you in the best possible position. You can see all of your options (as well as any incoming threats) and can therefore make a quick and well-informed decision about what to do next. And a first touch that settles the ball directly in front of you allows you to play the ball, with your very next touch, in whatever direction you decide is best.

This seemingly minor thing – how exactly you receive an incoming pass – is so crucial, I'm going to show you what it looks like if you do it wrong, to make absolutely sure you understand why it's so important to do correctly. Consider the same situation: you're the center back, the right fullback plays the ball diagonally backwards to you, the other team's forward is barreling toward you, and the left back is wide open to your left. You are doing a nice job of facing the space, i.e., in this situation, you are facing forward. But suppose that instead of letting the ball roll across your body and trapping it with your back foot, you control it with the outside (or bottom) of your front foot (i.e., the foot that is closer to where the ball is coming from) as shown in Figure 5C.

There are several things that you *could* do next. You could rotate your body slightly to the right and pass it immediately back to the right back who passed to you. But remember the situation. (See Figure 5A again if needed.) One of the black triangle players was coming hard at the right back. That's why she passed it backwards to you in the first place. So playing it immediately back to her is really dangerous! You probably don't want to do that. Another thing you could do is start dribbling (with a next touch pushing the ball back to the right or slightly forward). But, with the black triangle forward bearing down on you, the deepest defender, that is also extremely dangerous and ill-advised.

*Figure 5C: Suppose that, in the same situation we've been thinking about, you receive the ball with your front foot. (You could trap it with the outside of your right foot, as shown here. Or you could stomp on the ball with the bottom of your right foot. It's equally bad either way.) The question is, now what? To pass the ball to the open player to your left, you'll either need to take an extra touch or two to get the ball in front of you where you can kick it with the inside of your right foot, or you'll need to leave the ball where it is and do some kind of hokey pokey dance to your right. Either of these takes time... time you don't have, with the other team's forward running at you!*

What you *should* do in this situation, as we've said, is pass the ball quickly over to your wide open teammate, the left back. But this is one thing that it is just *physically impossible* to do, with any kind of urgency, with the ball on the outside of your right foot as in Figure 5C. You could rotate your body to the left, taking a couple of touches to bring the ball over to the left as you turn, and then pass. Or you could leave the ball where it is and take a step or two backwards and to the right, and then pass. But both of those things take time that you do not have.

So, if you receive the ball as pictured in Figure 5C, you make your one good option – passing the ball *quickly* to the left back – physically impossible. Only bad things, therefore, can result. So it really is crucially important to receive the ball correctly, with the back foot, as shown in Figure 5B.

And this is, of course, a general principle. When you are not already pressured, you should receive the ball, across your body, with the back foot, so that you can, if needed, pass the ball *quickly*, with your very next touch, in any of the directions you can see, because you are facing the space.

## 5.3  ⚽  Responsibilities of passer and receiver

The importance of receiving the ball in a certain way when it is passed to you places a certain responsibility on your teammate who is making that pass: your teammate must put the ball a little bit in front of you so that it is as easy as possible for you to receive it correctly.

And of course you are as often the passer as the receiver, so it might be helpful to restate the same point this way: when *you* pass the ball to a teammate, *you* must put the ball a little bit in front of her so it is as easy as possible for her to receive it correctly. Just vaguely kicking it in her general direction is not good enough. You should pass to your teammate's back foot!

(Notice, by the way, that this implies yet another way in which facing the right direction, and doing so *early*, is helpful: when you are looking to receive a pass, the way you are facing communicates to your teammate with the ball exactly where you want the pass to come in. So you should work to face the space even before the ball is on its way to you!)

I've just been saying what *should* happen. When your teammates pass to you, they *should* pass the ball directly to your back foot. And when you make a pass, you *should* pass the ball directly to your teammate's back foot. (At least, this is how passes to relatively stationary players should work. If someone is running, or has space to start running, passes should be more into the space in front of them.)

But, just like in real life, what *should* happen and what *does* happen are not always exactly the same thing. For a variety of reasons, passes won't always arrive exactly where they should.

If the pass is a little too far in front of you, it's obvious what you have to do: step forward as needed to get it. But what if the ball is instead a little bit behind you? Let's think about this again in the context of our familiar concrete example, with you playing the role of the center back receiving a diagonal backwards pass from the right fullback. Suppose the pass comes in a little behind you. The two frames of Figure 5D show two different ways you might control the ball after turning to your right so you can receive it: you could trap it with the outside of your left foot (left frame), or with the inside of your right foot (right frame). Which way of receiving the ball do

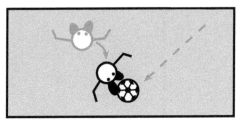

*Figure 5D: Suppose that, in the same situation we've been thinking about, the pass is a little behind you, so you have to turn to your right to control it. The two panels show two different ways you might then take a first settling touch on the ball. You could, as shown in the panel on the left, control it with the outside of your left foot. Or, as shown in the panel on the right, you could control it with the inside of your right foot. Which do you think is the better option?*

you think is best in this situation?

Seriously, take a minute and think about it before reading on.

Once you have an answer in mind, read on to see if we agree.

If your answer was "I'm not sure, it seems like they're both pretty bad" – that is exactly what I was thinking, too! It was actually a trick question. I think the best thing to do in this situation is *not* rotate your body to the right and then trap the ball in one of the ways shown in Figure 5D. Why not? Because then you're no longer facing the space and so all of the advantages of doing that that we've been talking about are out the window.

So what should you do instead of turning to receive the ball?

Simple: just *move backwards* (and/or to your right), but without rotating, so you are still facing the space and can still receive the ball in the proper way. See Figure 5E.

(Of course, if the pass is *so* far behind you that you can't just reposition yourself, by backpedaling or whatever, to receive it in the ideal way, you might have to turn and chase. Getting to the ball first is obviously the most important thing: it's better to get there first but facing in some non-ideal direction, than to let the black triangle forwards steal the ball and score. But if the pass is so inaccurate that you have to turn and chase, then you're

*Figure 5E: The best way to receive the ball, if the pass is a little bit behind where you wanted it, is shown here. Instead of turning, just backpedal and/or side-shuffle quickly and then receive it in the standard correct way: facing the space, and with your back foot!*

basically in the situation shown in Figure 1C. Just pass the ball back to the goalie – the only wide-open player in the direction you're now facing – and your team can start building again from there.)

To summarize, facing the space is extremely valuable. And receiving the ball with your back foot, so you can pass immediately, with your next touch if necessary, to any open teammate you can see, is also extremely valuable. Your teammates should always try to deliver their passes directly to your back foot, to make it as easy as possible for you to receive the ball correctly. And when you pass to them, you should return the favor. But receiving correctly is so important that you should be willing to work really hard to do it if at all possible – repositioning yourself as needed – even when the incoming pass is less than perfect.

# 5.4 ⚽ Stop it and go

The points we've been making so far about how to receive the ball (which way to face and which surface of which foot to use for your first controlling touch) apply most directly to players in the back (not just the center back we've been thinking about as an example, but also the goalie and the outside backs) and players out on the wings. For all of these players, "the space" that they generally want to face is the whole area of the field that all the players

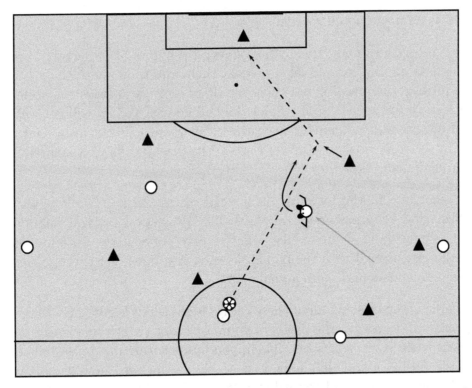

*Figure 5F: You are playing forward and get open for a nice forward pass from the center midfielder. You're even facing a really smart direction that allows you to see the incoming pass and also the direction you want to go with it, namely, toward the goal. But then you do something really foolish: you let the ball go right past you, and then fall in behind it to chase after it. But, inevitably, you can't accelerate nearly fast enough to get to the ball before a black triangle defender wins it and passes it smartly and safely back to her goalie. What a waste of a good goal-scoring opportunity!*

on both teams (with the possible exception of their own goalie) occupy.

But the situation can be a little different for players in the middle of the field or up front.

Let's get into thinking about this by starting with another one of my pet peeves. Consider the situation shown in Figure 5F. You are playing forward and you've done a great job of moving into a position where you are open to receive a nice forward-diagonal pass from one of the center midfielders behind you. How do you receive the ball?

Too often I see kids make the mistake shown (in Figure 5F): they don't really receive it at all, but instead let it go past them and then try to chase it. But this almost always results in a turnover. It takes several steps to accelerate, from rest, to top speed. So if you let the ball go past you, it will get way out ahead of you, and a defender from the other team will inevitably get to it first. In the scenario shown in the Figure, the defender plays it smartly back to her goalie, and now they have it instead of us.

What should you, the forward, do instead in this situation? You want to establish and keep possession of the ball. (Possession, as you might have heard, is precious.) But you also want to give yourself the option of going immediately forward with the ball and seeing if you can get through the gap between defenders and score a goal.

The perfect way of doing all of these things is shown in Figure 5G. First, you stop the ball dead with the inside of your back foot (which, in this situation, happens to be your right foot). Then, you immediately take a second touch, with the inside of your left foot, and accelerate forward now dribbling the ball through the gap and toward the goal. With a little practice, these two touches – stopping the ball to establish clean possession, and then getting it moving forward again just as you are accelerating forward yourself – can happen in rapid succession. Bang bang! The ball is moving forward almost as soon as it would have if you hadn't touched it at all.

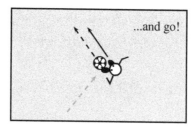

*Figure 5G: Close-up view of the "stop-it-and-go" maneuver. Your first controlling touch is with the inside of your back foot, as usual. (Here your "back foot" is your right foot because the ball is coming from your left.) Then you immediately push the ball forward with the inside of your other foot, as you simultaneously accelerate yourself to go forward with it.*

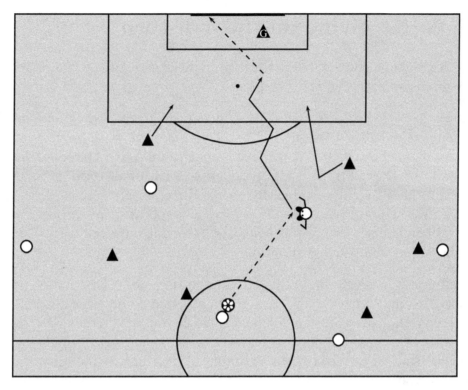

*Figure 5H: Instead of letting the ball go past you and then turning to chase it (which almost always results in a turnover), you should stop-it-and-go.*

But your touching it shifts everything else to your advantage. That first controlling touch makes it *yours*. Plus, when you now accelerate forward with it, you will naturally do so into a slightly different direction than the ball was originally going. That slight change of direction is something the defenders now have to react to, and that buys you some additional time.

Maybe you'll be able to dribble through the gap and score, as shown in Figure 5H. Or maybe the defenders close the gap in time so you slow it down and pass to one of your teammates who is yelling with her legs. Either way, your team keeps the ball and has the chance to develop a good scoring opportunity.

# 5.5 ⚽ Receiving on the half-turn

Let's think about how the stop-it-and-go maneuver relates to the principles we've discussed earlier in this Chapter.

Look again at Figure 5H, and notice in particular the way your body is oriented as the ball is coming: you're facing *sideways*, with your shoulders lined up parallel to the sidelines. This is sometimes called "receiving on the half-turn" or "receiving with an open body." (The "half-turn" means that you are rotated roughly 90° relative to the direction of the incoming ball.) But I find it helpful to recognize it as just the application of the ideas we've been talking about – facing the space and receiving with the back foot – in a slightly more complicated situation.

The situation is more complicated than the ones we talked about earlier because, in this scenario, you are right in the middle of the action. When you receive the ball in the middle of the field, you are literally surrounded by teammates, opposing players, and seams that you might dribble or pass through. It would be nice to be able to take in information about all of those things, so you could make a fully-informed decision about the best direction to go with the ball after you receive it. But although you can and should stay aware of what's going on behind you, by periodically looking back over your shoulder, you will always have better awareness of what's happening in front of you. And when you're in the middle of the field, it's impossible for everything to be in front of you.

That's why the "half-turn" orientation for receiving the ball, shown in Figure 5H, is so good. It allows you to receive the ball facing the space that includes the *most relevant* things: the incoming pass, and the forward direction you'd prefer to take the ball after you get it.

The point here is that receiving the ball in this way, on the half-turn, is great whether you specifically intend to dribble forward, as in the stop-it-and-go maneuver, or not. You can receive it on the half-turn and decide, on the fly, whether to dribble forward, make a forward-diagonal pass, dribble backwards because there is too much pressure ahead, etc. And this decision can be a smart, well-informed one because you have good vision of the relevant space.

Figure 5I shows another illustrative example. You are one of the center

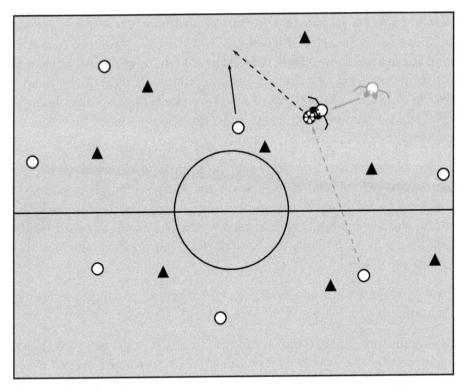

*Figure 51: The bread-and-butter play of a central midfielder. You find your way into a space between and behind two opposing players, and you recognize (by checking over your shoulder) that the deeper defender is not stepping forward to challenge for the ball as it comes. So you have enough time and space to settle the ball with your back foot, in the standard way, and then do something fun – e.g., you could dribble forward (using the stop-it-and-go maneuver) or, as shown here, immediately pass to another teammate who is making a nice aggressive gap-exploiting forward run.*

midfielders and do a nice job of yelling with your legs to get open for a seam-splitting pass from the right back. If you receive the ball on the half-turn, as shown, you can see very clearly when one of your teammates makes an aggressive forward run, and you can put the ball between the two black triangle defenders for her to run onto.

Note that the geometry of the passing sequence here (including the orientation of your body relative to your two teammates who are involved) is *exactly* the same as it was in the simpler example from earlier – the one shown in the lower frame of Figure 5A in which you were the center back, receiving a backwards-diagonal pass from the right back and then making a forward-diagonal pass to the left back on the other side of the field. It is exactly the same, that is, but *rotated*, so that the role played by the horizontal (left/right) directions in the earlier example is now played instead by the vertical (forward/backward) directions.

The lesson is that when you are near the middle of the field and receiving a forward pass, you should receive it on the half-turn (and, of course, with your back foot) for exactly the same reasons that the center back, in the earlier and simpler example, should receive the ball facing forward (and with the back foot). In both cases, this way of receiving provides the best way for you to face the space.

Let's see what you think about a related example involving one additional complication.

Suppose again that you are the center mid and find your way into that same nice seam behind the two black triangles. Your teammate makes the same aggressive forward run as in Figure 5I, but this time, as you are approaching the incoming ball and getting ready to receive it, the deeper black triangle defender shifts to the left (i.e., shifts to her right) to prevent that next pass, as shown in Figure 5J.

What do you think is the best way to receive the incoming pass in this situation?

Take a minute and think about that.

When you're ready, you can read on so we can compare answers.

Here's what I was thinking. By shifting her position, the deep black triangle defender really cuts off any good forward options near the middle of the field. The through-ball to your running teammate is no longer a good option (it'll just be intercepted) and dribbling that way would also be rather pointless.

But the same defensive shift that closes off opportunities in that one direction, opens opportunities up in another direction. In particular, there is suddenly a lot of juicy open space out on the right wing. So, if you can sense all of this and react quickly enough (no easy feat, to be sure, but it is possible

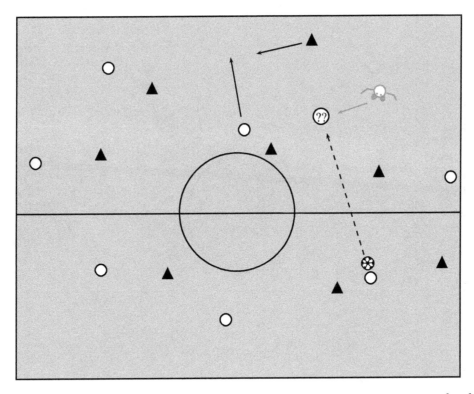

*Figure 5J: As you approach and prepare to receive the incoming pass, the deep black triangle defender moves to the left (i.e., to her right) in anticipation of the possible sequence of events shown in Figure 5I. What do you think is the best way to receive the ball?*

with practice) you can get to the spot to receive the incoming pass, but turn around, as it's arriving, so you can receive it on the half-turn but facing the opposite side of the field as before.

This is shown in Figure 5K.

The point that this example is meant to illustrate is a simple one: there are two sidelines! So, in the type of situation we've been thinking about, where you are receiving a forward pass near the middle of the field, the recommendation to receive the pass "on the half-turn" still leaves you with two options: you can be half-turned to face the left side of the field (as in Figure 5I) or half-turned to face the right side of the field (as in Figure 5K).

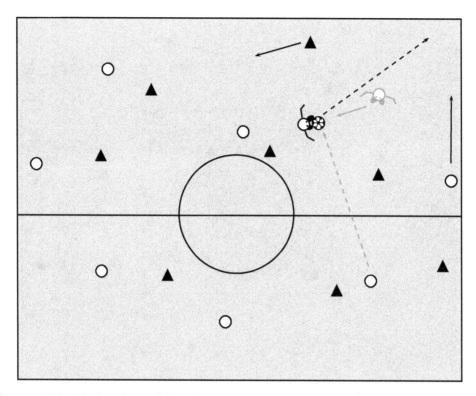

*Figure 5K: If the deep defender moves to her right (i.e., to the west) in anticipation of the possible sequence of events shown in Figure 5I, this opens up some juicy space where she was before, down the right wing. So now, when you receive the pass in that seam behind the other two defenders, it is better to "take it on the half turn" but facing the opposite direction as before (facing east instead of west). Then you can dribble or (even better!) play the ball into space for the right winger to run onto.*

Which side it is better to face in a given situation depends on a lot of factors, and can be difficult to decide correctly in the heat of the moment. No book can teach you to do this well. You just have to practice a lot to get good at it.

But a book can let you know that you face this choice, and hence motivate you to work on choosing well.

## 5.6 ⚽ Receiving under pressure

The examples from the last section show how, when you are receiving the ball in the middle of the action, the questions about which way it is best to face, and how exactly to receive the ball, get a little more subtle and complicated. If you can't be facing everything that's potentially relelvant, you have to make some kind of decision about which things are most important, and that is a bit subjective and a bit hard to decide in the heat of the moment.

And these issues only get cloudier when you are receiving in really tight spaces and/or with intense and immediate pressure. Let's just think about a couple of examples quickly.

First, let's return to the situation that we looked at to start this Chapter: you're the center back, receiving a diagonal backwards pass from the right back. When we thought about this before, we supposed that the black triangle forward was moving toward you and threatening pressure. This meant you had to move fast, if you wanted to get the ball over to your wide-open left back, before the pressure arrived. But it was at least possible to succeed at doing that, with the appropriately quick receive-and-pass combination of two touches.

Now imagine being in that same situation, but with the black triangle forward being a little closer and/or a little faster, such that she's likely to apply a bone-crunching tackle just as the ball is arriving at your feet, and hence probably win the ball away from you and score. In this case, you have to forget about which direction you're facing and which surface of which foot would otherwise have been ideal to control the ball with, and just do whatever you can to avoid that tackle and keep the ball for your team.

One good possibility is shown in Figure 5L: you step toward the incoming ball (giving yourself the best possible chance of getting to it first) and touch it to your right (i.e., toward the southeast), with the outside of your right foot. This is a good direction to push the ball, and a good part of your body to do it with, because it keeps your body between the ball and the marauding opponent. Using your body to shield the ball like this buys you another second and another touch, which, if all goes well, you can use to (for example) play the ball backwards to your keeper and escape the immediate danger.

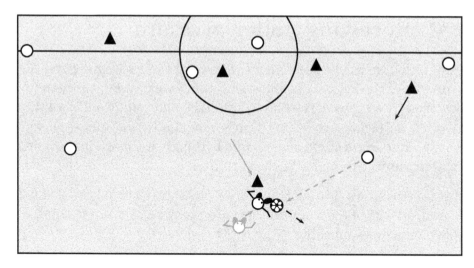

*Figure 5L: Suppose an opposing player is going to be right on top of you as you receive the pass, so you have to worry not only that she might steal the ball away, but that her method of doing so might put you in the hospital. In this case, you cannot simply stand your ground, facing the space and waiting for the ball to get to your back foot. You have to instead go into emergency mode, stepping toward the ball aggressively to make sure you get to it first, and then doing something to make sure your team keeps it. One good possibility is using your body to shield the ball and letting your first touch move it away from the immediate pressure, as shown. Note that this means your first touch on the ball will be with the outside of your front foot – the exact opposite of what we said before was ideal in the more standard, lower-pressure version of this situation. But it's OK. Desperate times call for desperate measures.*

Or maybe, instead of shielding and retreating, you can take advantage of the black triangle player's forward momentum by accelerating toward the ball, taking a first touch that pushes the ball back in the direction it was coming from, stepping quickly in that same direction (so the marauding opponent, who can't slow down or change direction quickly enough, runs right behind you), and then dribbling forward with the ball.

Lots of things are possible here, and it just takes a lot of experience to learn to read the situation and choose a good option. The only thing I can say to be helpful is this: if implementing "face the space" and "receive with your back foot" puts you in danger of getting mauled or robbed, it's appropriate to fall back to even more fundamental principles such as "possession is precious" or even "it's bad to have to be on crutches for the next six weeks because both of your ankles are broken."

## 5.7 ☺ Play the way you face

The theme of this Chapter is that, when you receive the ball, you should (to the greatest extent possible) already be facing the direction you want to play the ball into. But the converse is also true: you should play the ball into the direction you are already facing.

In normal, low-pressure situations, these aren't very different. You face the space, receive the ball, and then play it into some part of that space you were facing. But, as we saw in the last section, when you are under intense pressure you often have to give up on "face the space" and retreat to "possession is precious." That is, you end up with the ball, but facing in some weird direction that is *not* the direction you would have preferred to go had the pressure not been there.

The lesson here is: even if the way you are facing is not the direction you would have preferred to go, you must still play the way you face.

The situation shown earlier, in Figure 5L, illustrates the reason for this rule. To prevent the black triangles from getting the ball, you accelerated toward it and shielded it from the pressure. Now you have it (which is great!), but you are dribbling backwards (which is not the direction you would have preferred). Playing the way you face, in this situation, means: pass it back to your goalie. She is literally the only teammate you can see in this moment, she is wide open, and she has perfect vision of the entire field. So passing back to her is by far your best option.

If, instead, you try to turn back around with the ball, to look for a forward passing or dribbling option, you will be turning right into the black triangle forward. She will almost certainly steal the ball off your feet and, before you even know what hit you, dribble down and score.

Turning right into pressure like this is just too dangerous.

Another example is illustrated in Figure 5M. Here you are the center mid-

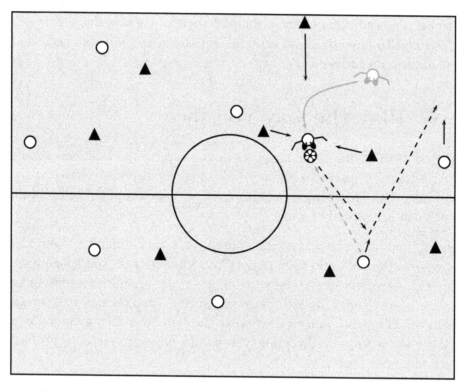

*Figure 5M: If the black triangles squeeze off the space you were hoping to receive the ball in, such that you can now only receive the pass running and facing backwards, as shown, you should probably just play the ball immediately back to the right back who passed to you. But the back-and-forth sequence was not unhelpful: the very motion of the black triangle players that prevented you from receiving the original pass in a more advantageous position, opens up new forward options like the pass to the right winger.*

fielder. But the black triangles foiled your plan to receive the ball in the seam behind the defenders: the defenders on either side of the seam pinched in (and the deeper defender also stepped up). So you moved toward the ball, along the seam, and received the ball. That's great! But now you have it, going and facing backwards, with two defenders right on your heels.

Here, again, you must resist the temptation to turn forward with the ball just on the grounds that you'd prefer to go forward. If you do that, you will lose it. And you don't want to lose it, because possession is precious.

Instead, you must play the way you face. You could dribble backwards for a bit and wait for a good passing option to open up. Or – the possibility that's illustrated in Figure 5M – you could one-touch the ball immediately back to the right back who passed it to you.

This often strikes players as the worst possible option, probably because it appears to put the team right back where they started. But appearances here are misleading! The very same defensive shift that prevented you from receiving the ball in a more advantageous position (namely, in the seam *behind* the defenders), opens up other opportunities elsewhere. One of those (sending the ball forward and wide for the right winger to run on to) is shown in Figure 5M.

Remember, although going forward and scoring goals is the ultimate aim, long-term possession is the way to achieve it. Turning right into pressure is a sure-fire way to lose possession. So just play the way you face, even if that's backwards, and even if it's directly back to the person who just passed to you. Keep the ball moving around and a good attacking opportunity will open up eventually.

One last point. So far, the two examples we've considered in this section involve you getting the ball, facing backwards, with pressure right on your heels. You *know* the defenders are behind you, so you *know* that turning around with the ball, to try to play it forward, means turning right into the defenders.

But what about a situation in which you receive the ball, facing backwards, and you have no idea what's behind you? (Of course, if you are doing a good job of facing the space, you should basically never find yourself in this situation. But, well, sometimes things happen.) The scenario – as you can picture it in your own mind – is shown in Figure 5N.

As far as you know, there *might* be nobody behind you. If you just turn with the ball, you *might* be able to dribble forward and score a glorious goal.

But there might also be two black triangle defenders right on your heels! The point is, if you aren't sure, you cannot take the risk. You have to assume the worst, and do something you're certain is safe.

Possession is precious, so play the way you face.

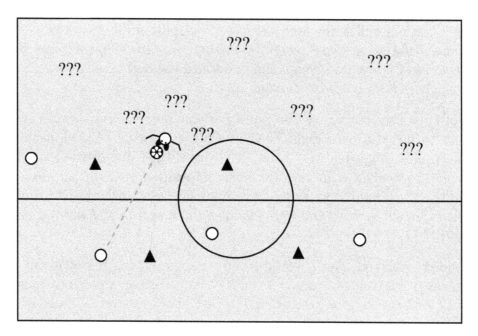

*Figure 5N: If you find yourself in a situation where you have the ball, facing backwards, but with no idea what is behind you, you must still play the way you face. Dribble or pass into the space you can actually see. Turning into the unknown with the ball is simply too risky.*

## 5.8 ⚽ Overview

As we discussed in Chapters 3 and 4, where you are on the field – relative to the sidelines, the goals, your teammates, your opponents, and the ball – is crucially important.

But your *orientation* – which direction you are facing – is also extremely important. It determines what you can see, and therefore what you know about, and therefore what information you have or don't have about what is about to happen. And it also determines what it is physically possible for you to do next with the ball.

In general, you want to orient yourself to acquire as much useful information as possible about the situation, so you can make the smartest possible choice about what to do next. Your teammate is passing you the ball, the ball is flying toward you, some of your other teammates are moving to get open for the next pass, defenders are shifting to cover them and apply pressure to you, and so on. You must make yourself aware of as much of this crucial action as possible. And you must keep the ball in front of you so you can play it quickly in a direction you're certain is both advantageous and safe.

You must, in short, face the space!

# CHAPTER 6

---

# Faster!

*"...the easiest way is often the hardest....  I see touching the ball once as the highest form of technique. But to be able to touch the ball perfectly once, you need to have touched it a hundred thousand times in training...."*

- Johan Cruyff

I N the next Chapter, Chapter 7, we will switch from talking about offense (what to do when your team has the ball) to defense (what to do when the other team has the ball). It is very difficult to choose just one last aspect of offense to highlight. There are so many important things that, in a much longer book, would surely warrant chapters to themselves.

For example: stop dribbling right into defenders! If you want to create scoring opportunities with your dribbling, forget about "beating" individual defenders in one-on-one battles, and instead attack the *gaps between* defenders! You want to avoid and get around (or between) defenders, not "go at them."

Or: trick the defense into reacting the wrong way by disguising what you are doing. Wind up for the 25-yard shot, but then dribble right around the defender and take the much higher percentage 15-yard shot instead. Square your hips as if you are going to pass in one direction, but then turn and put the ball where you really wanted it to go. With practice, you can even lie with your eyes: look to the right as you are preparing to pass to the left and vice versa.

Or: don't dribble the ball toward an open teammate! When you get to where he is, it's almost always unclear to both of you who should now take the ball, and even if it is clear who has it, you'll be in each others' way. Plus, by dribbling at an open teammate, you reduce your passing options, because you can't pass to someone who is right on top of you. For all of these reasons (and more), dribbling at an open teammate often results in a really pointless turnover. If you think it would help your team for somebody to have the ball over where the open teammate is, for heaven's sake just let him be the one to have it there: pass it to him, and then start working to get open for the subsequent pass.

But all of these sorts of things can be practiced and developed on the training field.

There is, however, one more "big picture" idea that I want to stress in this Chapter, and that is the importance of *speed*. This has been mentioned already several times, but (somewhat paradoxically) it deserves a slower and more careful discussion.

## 6.1 ⚽ Why do we pass?

I have been a proponent of a certain style of play – involving quick, accurate, on-the-ground passing – for as long as I can remember. Partly this is because the better coaches I had as a kid already advocated this style. Partly it's because, as an amateur soccer player, I know it is just more *fun* to play quality team soccer (as opposed to watching some annoying hotshot do everything himself, and also as opposed to *being* the annoying hotshot). But mostly it's because as a fan of professional soccer, and as a coach of my kids' teams, and as an amateur player, I have seen that this style is not only beautiful and fun, but also ruthlessly effective.

Still, it was only about a year ago that I overheard a conversation between my older son's team and his coach, that profoundly deepened my understanding of the style of soccer I love. The coach paused a keepaway game, where they had been practicing passing the ball around quickly and efficiently, and asked the kids: "Why do we pass?"

After an awkward silence, one player offered up: "To move the ball around?" The coach stayed silent and let everybody ponder that for a minute. Standing on the sideline, I was also pondering. Over the next few seconds my thoughts went from "yes, exactly!" to "wait, but what is the point of moving the ball around?" The player's answer wasn't really an answer at all: "passing" and "moving the ball around" are just two different ways of describing the same thing.

Anyway, after a few more seconds, the coach finally offered up his answer, which (I am embarrassed to admit!) was a revelation. (You'd think I would have already understood the *point* of the thing I had been teaching my kids for years...) Anyway, his answer was: "to move the *defense* around."

Ah... right.

You see, the defense is trying to prevent your team from scoring. At any given moment, the guy with the ball is the most immediate threat, and so the defense arranges itself to guard against that threat: somebody steps to the ball to apply pressure and other defenders drop into supporting ("covering") positions, just in case the guy with the ball slips past that first defender. After these defensive rearrangements (which take only a second or two), the thing (namely the guy with the ball) that *was* the most immediate threat is now the *least* threatening thing!

As both a coach and a player, I always find it extremely frustrating when a player on my team receives the ball in what could be a threatening position, and then just holds it for one ... two ... three ... four seconds – looking around, testing out some fancy footwork moves he practiced last week, contemplating his options, etc. Finally, after this excruciating delay, he tries to dribble forward to create a scoring opportunity. But by then it is simply too late. The defenders have already shifted into good positions to eliminate this threat. It's now basically the situation pictured in Figure 1B, and dribbling forward inevitably results in a turnover.

But if the team with the ball passes it around more quickly than the defense can react – if nobody holds onto it for those pointless and excruciating two ... three ... four seconds – then the defenders have a tough time of it. They are constantly trying to get into good positions, but never quite managing to get there before they have to react again in a different direction. The result is that gaps open up, players get forgotten about in the chaos and left unmarked, and the team with the ball can find much easier, much higher-percentage chances to score goals.

There is, in short, an inherent value in speed. Whatever exactly you are going to do eventually with the ball, the faster you can do it, the better.

## 6.2 ⚽ Fewer touches is better

One straightforward application of this idea – which is trivially easy to express in words, but the work of a lifetime to implement well – is that the fewer touches you can take on the ball, to accomplish some task, the better.

The reason is simple. Touches take time, and taking time is the enemy of speed.

There's really not much else to say about this. Decide what to do and then do it. Don't hold onto the ball for no reason. If somebody's open in a good position and you're going to pass to them, or if you have an opening and are going to shoot, pull the trigger immediately. Don't wait. And practice, practice, practice to improve your individual technique. Learn to settle the ball with your first touch no matter how it comes at you, and then learn to do with one touch what previously took two, by using your first touch to not only settle the ball but also get it moving in the direction you are going next.

## 6.3 ⚽ The big race

A couple of years ago, when the kids I coach were a little younger, I started practice one day by letting the kids race each other. I set up some cones about 30 yards from the sideline and had an assistant stand by them (nominally) to make sure the kids followed the rules. Then, in groups of three or four, the kids raced: run across, touch a cone, and run back. The winners of each preliminary heat made it to the finals, and we determined the top three fastest runners on the team, in order.

Then the real fun began. I gave the fastest player on the team a ball and said "now do it dribbling." We re-ran the finals race, and the kid who had previously been the fastest – but who was now required to dribble the ball as he went – now came in last place.

The lesson, of course, was that you can run faster without the ball than you can run with the ball. And that is really important. It's why, for example, the give-and-go sequence shown back in Figure 4F is so much better than just dribbling up the sideline. Pass, move, and get the ball back, and you end up having it there sooner than if you had dribbled it there.

But there was one more lesson to come. I took the ball and joined the kids on the sideline. This time I invited all of them to join the race again. I leaned over the ball like I was getting ready to get a fast start. I wanted them to think I was going to try to dribble the ball, down and back, to see if I could beat all of them. They were excited for that challenge now that they knew other kids could beat the fastest kid, if the fastest kid was handicapped by having to dribble the ball. This might be their chance to finally be faster than the coach!

But when I said "Go!" I didn't dribble the ball at all. I just stood up straight, passed the ball over to my assistant by the cones, and then he calmly passed it back to me. It wasn't even close: the ball made it across and back before the kids had even taken ten steps toward the other side.

So they learned another lesson: nobody – not you, not me, not Usain Bolt – is even remotely close to being fast enough to keep up with a crisply-passed ball.

And that means, if there's some kind of good attacking opportunity some-where on the field, and our team needs to get the ball over there to try to take advantage of it before the defense has time to react, we are far, far better off passing it over there, than dribbling it there.

If faster is better than slower, then passing is better than dribbling.

## 6.4 ☺ The nature of speed

"Speed" is a broad abstraction that combines a number of different elements and factors.

As mentioned earlier, one aspect of it primarily has to do with your individual technique. There are certain basic maneuvers that you'll need to perform over and over again in soccer – for example, settling an incoming pass to your feet so you can make the next pass. You have to learn to perform these operations *properly* (so that, for example, additional corrective touches are not required) and (relatedly but not identically) *quickly*. This is what training sessions are for.

Another obvious element of speed is physical: how fast can you run? If, for example, you are the winger in Figure 4F, a lot depends on how quickly you can get down the sideline to receive the return pass from the center midfielder. If you get there soon enough, you'll be able to get by and get behind the black triangles' left wing. But if you run more slowly (because your top speed just isn't that good, or because you're jogging instead of sprinting) you'll get there too late and that particular attacking opportunity will never develop.

Physical speed is also something you can improve. There are ways to increase your top (sprinting) speed with training, and of course you can improve your overall conditioning so you have the energy to sprint instead of jogging even late in the second half of the game.

But the main point I want to stress here is that a hugely important and under-appreciated element of speed is neither technical nor physical, but *mental*. Johan Cruyff made the point this way:

> "Speed is often confused with insight. When I start running earlier than the others, I appear faster."

But, I would say, this is not merely an appearance. Speed – in the sense in which speed actually matters – is about when you complete the task: when the ball leaves your foot, safely on its way to a teammate in a better position, for example, or when you arrive at that spot where the return pass is waiting for you.

Winning the race means getting to the finish line first. In 100 meter dashes, for example, everybody has to start at the same time. So getting to the finish line first requires you to have gone the fastest in the purely physical sense. But the races that occur in soccer are just not like that. There is no rule saying that you are not allowed to start moving, to get open for the next pass or whatever, until your defender also starts moving. You can start whenever you want. So why not give yourself the biggest head-start possible, to dramatically increase the chances that you win?

You can and you should. But then you can see why this aspect of speed is not physical, but mental. To give yourself a head-start, you have to know what direction to go – you need to sneak a few early steps in the direction of the finish line, not the opposite way! You need, in short, to be able to *anticipate* what is going to happen next, what your role in it could and should be, and start getting yourself into position, *right now*, to play that role.

I am not going to give a bunch of examples here, because literally the whole book up to this point has been full of them. Indeed, helping you with this mental element of speed – helping you to be able to identify what is happening now and anticipate what needs to happen next – is the entire point of this book. The hope is that by having a deeper and broader abstract understanding of certain key principles of quality soccer, you will be better able to recognize what you should be doing next, hence better able to take a head-start on doing it.

## 6.5 ⚽ Always engaged

As a short and slightly stocky fellow, I find the importance of the mental aspect of speed liberating and inspiring. You don't have to be six-foot-four, with abs of steel and a new $800 haircut every three days, to be a brilliant soccer player. You just have to play a little smarter than the next guy. And, frankly, that is not too hard. Have you *seen* the next guy??

But actually "smarter" isn't quite the right word. What it takes is to be constantly *engaged*, mentally, with the game – constantly using your eyes and your brain to identify what's going on, anticipate what will happen next, and give yourself as many little head-starts as possible. You need to be constantly asking and answering questions:

*"What is happening? Where am I? Should I get wider so I'm more open and have more time and space if the ball comes to me? Should I drop back to provide better support for my teammate with the ball? Should I move toward the ball to make sure my teammate can get it to me? Should I push forward and call for a through-ball? Where is the ball going to go next? If it comes to me, what am I going to do with it? Which direction will the pressure come from? If the pass goes to someone else, am I open for an immediate one-touch next pass? Will my teammate know I'm open? Will the ball coming to me make the defense react in a way that opens up a seam that I can exploit with another quick pass? If my teammate takes a shot and there's a deflection or rebound, where is the ball likely to end up?"*

You get the idea.

Let me try to concretize this at least a little bit by recalling some of the situations we've encountered in earlier chapters.

Flip back and compare, for example, the positioning of the left winger in Figures 3A and 3B. We talked before about why it's better for the left winger to stay wide, as in Figure 3A. The point here is, he has to *already* be wide, as the ball is going from the center mid on the right to the center back (or the other center mid or the forward). If the left winger has gotten sucked in toward the middle of the field, say where he is shown in Figure 3B, and only realizes, as the ball is on its way (say) from the center mid to the center back, it is too late. The center back will look up as the ball is coming to him and either see a left winger who is too close to him and not open, or a left winger who is running, inexplicably from his point of view, directly away from him. Either way, the center back will immediately veto passing to the left wing, and move on to consider some other option.

This lost opportunity represents a failure, by the left wing, to be mentally engaged. He let himself get sucked into a less advantageous position, for no particular reason, but instead just because he wasn't really thinking about what he was doing.

In this case, the mental engagement required by the left winger consists largely of resisting the temptation to move out of an already advantageous position, by identifying exactly how and why it is advantageous:

> "*Should I move toward the ball to make sure my teammate can get it to me?* No! There are no black triangles within 40 yards of me out here, so somebody will be able to get it to me when the moment is right. *Should I push forward and call for a through-ball?* No. Better to bide my time here and let the pass go into the space in front of me so I can receive it with a head of steam. *If the next pass goes to someone else, am I open for an immediate one-touch next pass? Will my teammate know I'm open?* Yes, if it's the center back or the forward, who can see me over here, but maybe not if it goes into the other center mid. If it goes to him, I might need to drop so he can see me. *Will the ball coming to me make the defense react in a way that opens up a seam that I can exploit with another quick pass?* Yes, quite possibly – as the defenders follow the ball over to my side, the closer ones will probably hustle faster than the farther ones, and some big gaps might open up in the middle. I'll keep my eyes open for a possible seam-splitting through-ball to our forward as I'm dribbling!"

That is what mental engagement sounds like in the privacy of your own mind.

Or: consider again the situation shown in Figure 3D. The black triangles just took a long, low-percentage, ill-advised shot which our goalie easily controlled and he now has the ball at his feet. Figure 3D shows the outside backs (and wingers) just standing there, in positions that were OK a couple seconds before when the other team had the ball, but which are now pretty useless. I drew and included that Figure because I wanted to show clearly how and why the positioning of the outside backs (and wingers) becomes problematic once our team gets the ball.

The point here, though, is that the situation shown in Figure 3D should never occur in the first place. It should never happen that the shot goes in and rolls slowly to the keeper's feet, he takes one controlling touch, and then looks up only to see his outside backs and wingers standing there, like zombies, near the middle of the field, staring back at him. It should not be necessary for the goalie (or a coach from the sidelines) to yell at those players: "Hey, maybe now would be a good time to think about spreading wide so we can start moving the ball forward!"

Instead, the moment it becomes clear that the goalie will get the ball at his feet (i.e., the moment it becomes clear that there is no chance of a deflection and a subsequent loose ball in front of the goal), the outside backs (and wingers) should be running – probably backpedaling so they can face the space as they move – into the positions shown in Figure 3E. They have to anticipate what is going to happen next, understand where they need to be to make that next thing work as well and as quickly as possible, and take the biggest possible head-start for themselves.

## 6.6 ⚽ Attitude matters

One last point. Part of mental engagement has to do with your attitude and in particular your ability to stay focused on how you can help your team create the next good opportunity, rather than getting bogged down with unhelpful negative emotions when something doesn't go quite the way you hoped.

For example, maybe you are playing left wing and doing a really nice job of staying wide. The center mid makes a nice backwards-diagonal pass to the center back, as in Figure 3A, but instead of one-touching the ball to the space out in front of you (so that you can implement your whole big plan about getting to it with a head of steam, dribbling forward to suck the defenders over, and then making a killer pass between defenders, for an easy finish by your center forward), the center back inexplicably boots the ball forward to nobody and the other team, unsurprisingly, ends up with it.

Or maybe you're the right back and, after you stole the ball away from him, the black triangles' forward hacked your ankles from behind as you were passing it back to your goalie. You turn to look at the ref expecting him to make the obvious call, but he just shrugs at you and says "play on!" What the heck! Is he blind, or just stupid?!

Or maybe you're the left forward in the situation shown in Figure 3J. You really wanted the center forward to pass the ball to you, but instead he passed it the other way. So you give up, check out mentally, turn around, and walk backwards (instead of making the forward run that, as shown in the Figure, would have resulted in your scoring a beautiful goal).

In all these kinds of situations – and, sadly, they do and will always occur – how you react to some frustrating turn of events can make a huge difference to your team's prospects for success.

We can put the point this way: the slowest and therefore most useless player on the field is the one with drooped head and shoulders who is pouting because he didn't get the ball or the call, or the one who is completely disengaged from the game because he's yelling at a teammate for doing something stupid.

Frustrating things will happen. Expect it and prepare yourself in advance to just get over them as quickly as possible. Speed matters here too.

And by the way, if *you* make a mistake that results in a turnover – e.g., your attempted pass to a teammate is off-target and gets intercepted – you should, as I said to my son recently, "apologize with your legs." That is, don't stand there and apologize to your teammate while the black triangles zoom down the field and score. Instead, run as fast as you can to apply pressure and try to win the ball back for your team.

Trust me, the rest of your team will appreciate that much more than any apology you could give with your mouth.

## 6.7 ⚽ Overview

Playing fast prevents the defense from setting up in good positions. It thus creates good attacking opportunities for your team.

But playing fast is not easy.

It requires good individual technique (e.g., the ability to control and pass the ball quickly and efficiently with the minimum number of touches, and the ability to receive the ball correctly to prevent turnovers and open up opportunities). It requires that when you move to a more advantageous position, you run fast. It requires that we move the ball around the field with quick, sharp passes, without anybody slowing things down by holding the ball too long and dribbling too much. And, most importantly, it requires full mental engagement so that, whatever you are doing next, you give yourself the biggest possible head-start.

Working to play *faster* – by improving the technical, physical, and especially mental aspects of your game – is probably the best way to improve your overall quality as a player.

Faster, simply put, is better. So if you want to be better, learn to be ... faster!

# CHAPTER 7

---

# Pressure With A Purpose

*"An example. When putting pressure on a right-footed defender, I would close him down on his right, forcing him to pass with his weaker left foot."*

- Johan Cruyff

EVERYBODY who has gotten this far into this book knows, already, that when the other team has the ball, it is important for one person to step to the ball-carrier and apply pressure. The reason for this is simple and obvious: if nobody applies pressure on the ball, the person with the ball will just dribble down and score. And we don't want that.

This chapter is all about how to apply pressure in the most effective possible way. The theme (which will very much continue over into the following Chapter, which discusses whole-team defense) is that the "first defender" – the person who steps to the ball to apply pressure – can do this in ways that accomplish more than just not letting the player with the ball dribble down and score.

But let's start with some basics.

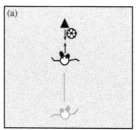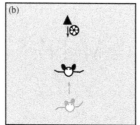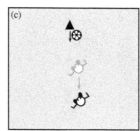

*Figure 7A: Three possible ways of approaching the ball-carrier to apply pressure. In frame (a) you close down the space as rapidly as possible by running directly at the player with the ball. You hope, of course, to steal the ball from him as soon as you get there. In frame (b), you approach more cautiously and then stop and try to set up as wide a barrier as possible when you reach a reasonable distance. In frame (c) you close down the distance initially, but then begin to retreat (keeping an approximately constant distance from the ball-carrier as he moves forward, and keeping your center of gravity low). Which approach do you think will be most effective and why?*

# 7.1 ⚽ None shall pass

Suppose, to start with the simplest possible case, that you are the defender in a 1v1 situation. You step to the player with the ball to apply pressure in a situation where, if he gets around you, he will almost certainly score a goal.

It is clear, then, that your number one priority must be to not let him get past you.

So, how should you approach the player with the ball to apply pressure and make it as difficult as possible for him to get around you? Let's do this pop-quiz style again. Figure 7A shows three different ways you might approach the application of pressure. In frame (a), you run as fast as you can at the player with the ball with the aim of initiating pressure (and maybe stealing the ball away) as quickly as possible. In (b) you approach more cautiously and stop before you get there, using your body to make the widest possible wall perpendicular to the direction the ball-carrier wants to go. Finally, in (c), you initially approach the ball-carrier but then back off and move backwards to maintain a constant distance as the ball-carrier moves forward.

Which method of initiating pressure do you think will be most effective and why?

Take a minute to come up with your own answer and then read on to hear what I think.

Option (a) may appear to have the virtues of aggressiveness and speed, but (especially against relatively skilled opponents) is almost always too aggressive. Typically the only thing that happens fast if you try to initiate pressure this way is that the ball-carrier uses your forward momentum against you by simply stepping (with the ball) to the side, letting you run right past. And then he continues forward and scores.

How about option (b)? The idea of building a wall may sound appealing but is completely wrong-headed in this case (and some others). To begin with, the very thing that makes your body shape wall-like is highly problematic. The flat, spread-out stance makes it almost impossible for you to move and react quickly if the ball-carrier changes directions. Any reasonably good player will go right around you almost every time if you hunker down in this way.

(There is also the additional problem that down at ground-level where the ball is, your "wall" actually consists of two widely-separated narrow posts, i.e., your legs. A skilled dribbler can and will therefore skip the scenic route and put the ball directly through the giant gap in the middle of your pathetic "wall.")

What about option (c)? It may seem like, if you approach the ball-carrier this way, you are not really applying pressure at all – you're just letting him move forward and moving with him as he goes. That is true, but nevertheless this is without question the proper way to initiate pressure here. Remember the situation: you are the only defender in the area, so if the person with the ball gets past you, he's going to score.

With option (c), you give up a little bit of yardage as you retreat, but by keeping a buffer between you and the ball-carrier, you buy yourself time to react if he suddenly changes speed or direction. Your 45°-rotated body orientation, with one foot somewhat forward and the other somewhat back, also gives you the ability to react much more quickly, shuffling backwards and/or side-to-side as needed, to stay between the ball-carrier and the goal.

As with so many things in soccer, it is really all about time. The point here is not that you shouldn't really challenge the ball-carrier and try to win the ball away. The point is rather that you need to buy yourself time to pick the proper moment to strike. If you just run straight in willy-nilly, as in (a), he'll get by you, and if you hunker down and wait for him to just bring the ball to you, as in (b), you will wait in vain. So get into a good position to stay in front of the player with the ball, as he moves, and wait for him to make a sloppy touch or an ill-advised turn. Then you can pounce and steal or poke the ball away.

And, honestly, even if that sloppy touch never comes, and you just wait him out, that's good too. As we talked about (from the opposite team's point of view) in the last Chapter, one player holding the ball for a long time is a terrible thing for the team with the ball and a great thing for the team without the ball: the one ... two ... three ... four seconds gives other defenders time to recover back and help out.

## 7.2 ⚽ Force to the outside

Option (c) from the last section is the basic, no-frills, vanilla way of initiating pressure. You should always do it like that. But you can and should do more. This section and the following several sections will introduce some of the additional secondary purposes that you can achieve while pressuring.

Frame (c) of Figure 7A shows you rotated about 45° to the left (i.e., counter-clockwise) relative to the (bad!) "flat wall" orientation you're shown as taking in frame (b). Note that you are also shifted a little bit to the right, so that the ball-carrier's path forward is a little more open to your left (his right). This combination of turning to the left and shifting to the right discourages the attacking player from trying to go around you to your right (his left): from his point of view, that path is just more blocked off, so he will tend to go instead to your left. This is just what you want, because that is the way you are facing. So by forcing – luring – him into going the way you want, you keep him in front of you and avoid any potentially dangerous surprises.

But why rotate left and shift right? As far as the situation in Figure 7A is concerned, it would be just as good to rotate right and shift left, and force/lure the attacker to your right instead.

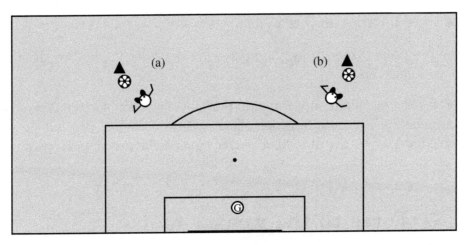

*Figure 7B: The first defender should generally apply asymmetrical pressure that makes the ball-carrier take the ball further to the outside. Thus (a) if the ball carrier is on the left side of the field, the first defender should "rotate left and shift right" to force/lure the ball-carrier to go to even further to the left. On the other hand (b) if the ball carrier is on the right side of the field, the first defender should "rotate right and shift left" to force/lure the ball-carrier to go even further to the right. In both cases, we want to force the player with the ball toward the nearest sideline, away from the more dangerous area in the center of the field.*

All other things being equal, you just have to arbitrarily pick one of these two equally-good mirror-image options.

But in a real game situation, all other things are never equal. There will always be some reason (and, actually, several, potentially conflicting reasons!) to force the attacker to one side as opposed to the other.

The simplest such factor has to do with where you are on the field. It is more dangerous for the attacking player to have the ball in the area right in front of the goal, than to have it out on the sides. It's just harder to score from out on the sides because the goal doesn't look as big from there.

Therefore, if the ball-carrier on whom you are initiating pressure is already on the left side of the field, you should always try to force/lure him to go even further to your left, i.e., toward the nearest sideline. And if the ball-carrier is already on the right side of the field, you should always try to force/lure him to go even further to your right.

See the positions taken up by the pressuring defender in the two situations shown in Figure 7B.

So that is the first of our supplemental purposes that you should always have in mind when you are the first defender: initiate pressure, yes, but do so in the way that pushes the attacking player toward the less dangerous outside areas of the field.

## 7.3 ⚽ Force to the weaker foot

If the player with the ball is near the middle of the field, it may not be clear which direction is toward the outside. But in this situation it doesn't really matter anyway. There is a different asymmetry that you, as the first defender, can exploit to shift things dramatically in your favor.

The fact is, most soccer players are not equally good with both feet. Most are right-footed, meaning that they can dribble, pass, and (of particular relevance here) shoot *way* better with their right foot than with their left foot. And of course there are also some people who are left-footed, i.e., for whom shots taken with the left foot are likely to be more powerful and more accurate than shots taken with the right foot.

The practical upshot of this fact is pretty obvious: if you are pressuring a player who has the ball in the dangerous area in front of the goal, and it's likely that, no matter what you do, he's going to find a way to get off a shot on goal, you should make him take that shot with his weaker foot! So, for example, if the attacking player is right-footed (which is probably, but not necessarily, the case), you should take up a defensive position like the one shown in Figure 7C.

Note that forcing the attacker to his weaker side requires that you know which side that is. Of course, right-footedness is more common than left-footedness. So if you just aren't sure, it is usually good to go with the odds and force the attacker to his left (your right) as shown in Figure 7C. But really you should not have to guess. If/when you are playing a defensive position, identifying the footedness of the attacking player(s) you are up

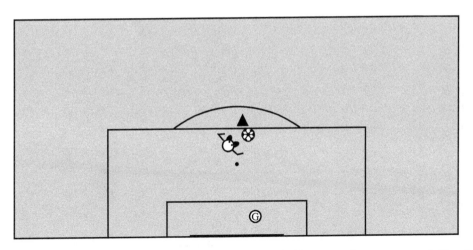

*Figure 7C: If the attacking player has the ball near the center of the field (such that neither sideline is meaningfully closer, and such that he's likely to be able to take a shot on goal), you should force the attacker to his weaker side so that, if and when he does take that shot on goal, he has to take it with his weaker foot. So, for example, if the attacking player is right-footed, you should position yourself as shown so that the attacker can only shoot on goal with his left foot.*

against is a basic requirement of the job. It's one of the first things you should do when you enter the game.

Let me finally just say that this secondary purpose – forcing players to their weaker side – is incredibly effective. I mean, it's almost embarrassing how effective it is. A huge fraction of players simply will not even attempt a shot with their weaker foot, because they know it will be weak and inaccurate. So if that's the only option you give them, they will do all kinds of crazy things. Some will dribble out of the danger area (which is great – crisis averted!). Some will just hold onto the ball making repeated (but, if you keep doing your job, hopeless) attempts to get around to your other side, like some kind of malfunctioning robot.

You basically have the power, as the first defender, to neutralize the attacker's biggest and best (and in many cases *only*) weapon.

This is a power you should use proudly and frequently.

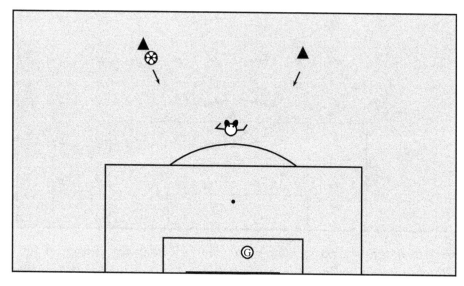

*Figure 7D: Two black triangle players are bringing the ball down against you, the one lone defender. What do you do? And what is up with your teammates today? They are really leaving the hard work to you over and over again here!*

## 7.4 ⚽ Take away the pass

So far we've been talking about what you can do, in addition to just applying generic vanilla pressure, to put yourself and your team in the best possible position when you are the lone defender in a one-on-one type situation.

But what if two or more attackers are coming at you? Consider for example the 2-v-1 scenario shown in Figure 7D. Besides trying to keep your panic in check, what should you do?

Well, let's think it through. First of all, you have to apply pressure to the ball-carrier. His first-choice option, surely, would be to just dribble down and score. So you have to apply some pressure and try to take that option away.

But given that you're going to initiate pressure against the ball-carrier, which way should you force him?

To decide, we have to think about the ball-carrier's second-choice option.

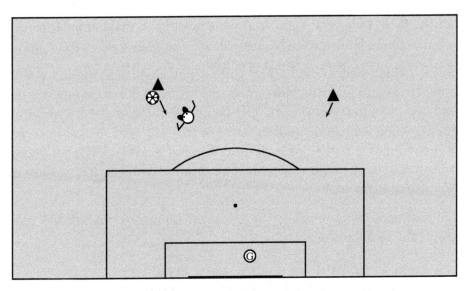

*Figure 7E: If you pressure the ball in the way that is shown here, you can try to cut off the pass at the same time you are forcing the ball-carrier wide and waiting for him to make a mistake so you can pounce and win or clear the ball.*

Basically, he wants to make sure he and his teammate maintain good horizontal separation, wait until you commit over to his side, and then pass the ball across to his now wide-open teammate who can put the ball into the back of the net.

(Notice that the situation here is exactly the same as the one we thought about before, back in Chapter 3. See Figure 3I. It's just that now we're thinking about it from the point of view of the defending team.)

Obviously, this is not a great situation to be in for the white circles team. If the black triangles play their cards right, they should probably be able to score. But often it is possible for a single defender to simultaneously take away the ball-carrier's best two options. Which is nothing to sneeze at.

The way to do this is shown in Figure 7E. Pressure the ball in the way we've been talking about and, in particular, force the ball-carrier to the outside, as shown. Depending on the exact positioning of the two black triangle players, it is often possible to achieve everything we talked about achieving in the 1-v-1 situation (namely, pressure the ball-carrier, force him to the outside areas of the field, bide your time, and wait for him to make a mistake so you can pounce) *and*, simultaneously, also cut off the pass to the other player.

This is not guaranteed to work. The ball-carrier might understand what you are trying to do and play the ball across, out in front of his teammate, before you get close enough to prevent it. Or the player without the ball might slow his run, dropping a little behind the level of the ball, and force you to rotate around even farther to the right if you want to prevent the pass to him – which then makes it much easier for the original ball-carrier to blow right past you toward the goal.

Still, simultaneously pressuring the ball and trying to cut off the pass, is probably your best option.

## 7.5  ⚽  Force toward your support

In more complicated situations, even more factors come into play.

For example, consider the 3-v-2 situation shown in Figure 7F, where it is the black triangle player in the middle who has the ball.

(This, incidentally, is the most interesting case because it is the most advantageous situation for the attackers. If one of the black triangles on the wing has the ball, it's more obvious what the defenders should do: the defender who is closer to the ball should apply pressure and, in particular, force to the outside, while the other defender stays central in support. This is why, when you find yourself in the happy situation of being one of the three in a 3-v-2 situation, you should usually pass the ball to the guy in the middle as early as possible, or just dribble into the middle while your two teammates fall into the lanes on either side of you.)

It should be clear that one of the two defenders needs to step to the ball and initiate pressure. And the symmetry of the situation suggests that it doesn't really matter which defender does this. Somebody just has to be the first to take the initiative, say "I got ball," and go to it.

Suppose you do this. Which way should you force and what position should your teammate take up in support?

As in the 2-v-1 situation we discussed previously, you can simultaneously

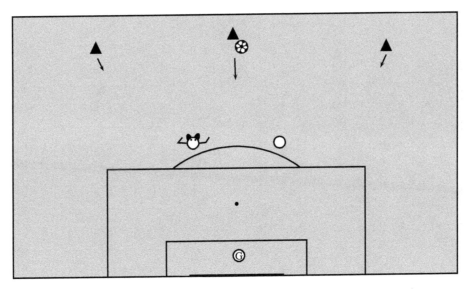

*Figure 7F: How should you and your teammate work together to try to repel the 3-person attack?*

pressure the ball and attempt to prevent a pass to one of the ball-carrier's teammates. In particular, you could "force right" and simultaneously prevent the pass to the attacker on the left side of the field. Or you could "force left" and simultaneously prevent the pass to the attacker on the right side of the field.

How to choose between these options?

It's your teammate – the second defender – who breaks the symmetry here. Since you happened to be the one to initiate pressure on the ball, and you happened to start more to the left, when you pressure the ball, your fellow defender will be behind you and *to your right*. And so this is the direction you should force, as shown in Figure 7G.

(If *he* had instead been the one to step first to the ball, he would want to force the ball-carrier to the *left*, instead, because that's where you are.)

So, in cases where there is a second defender, the first defender should generally try to force the player with the ball to the side where the second defender offers some defensive support. For example, in the situation pictured in Figure 7G, if the attacker with the ball gets past you (on the side

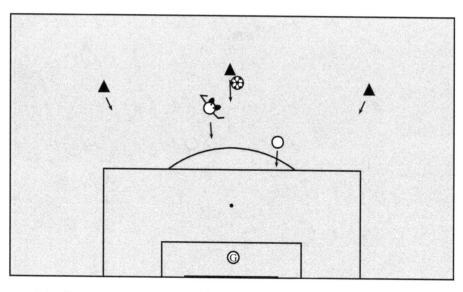

*Figure 7G: In a 3-v-2 situation (in which the attacking player in the middle has the ball) the first defender should force to whichever side the second defender is on.*

you are allowing/encouraging him to try to go to) – *or* if he passes to the teammate your positioning allows him to pass to – then your teammate, the second defender, is in a good position. He can step to whichever attacker has the ball and engage in the defensive tactics we discussed before.

And as long as the attacker does not get by you and you manage to successfully prevent the pass to the player on the side that you are trying to force away from (i.e., the player on the left of Figure 7G), you effectively take that third attacker out of the picture, and thus reduce the 3-v-2 situation to a more manageable 2-v-2.

## 7.6 ⚽ Overview

When the other team has possession and you are the closest to the player with the ball, you should step up and apply pressure. Your first priority is always to prevent the player with the ball from getting past you. Turning your body 45°, making your center of gravity low, and shuffling backwards to keep a several-yard buffer between you and the ball-carrier are helpful.

As you do this, you can patiently wait for the ball-carrier to make a sloppy touch or other mistake so you can pounce and challenge hard for the ball.

But, as we have seen in the several example scenarios, there are other things you can accomplish with your pressure as well. You can force the ball-carrier to a less dangerous, outside position on the field. You can force him to shoot with his weaker foot (or, perhaps, not at all). You can try to eliminate one of his passing options. And you can force him in a direction where you have one or more teammates in supporting defensive positions.

So, whenever you pressure the ball, do it in a way that allows you to accomplish one or more of these other goals. Pressure with a purpose!

# CHAPTER 8

---

# D As One

*"I like to turn traditional thinking on its head, by telling the striker that he's the first defender, by helping the goalkeeper to understand that he is the first attacker.... You do that effectively by keeping your eye on each other. So as soon as one player starts running, the other one tracks him."*

- Johan Cruyff

WE have said, and it is certainly true, that the aim of defense is to prevent the other team from scoring. But it is helpful to re-interpret the purpose of defending in terms of the fundamental principle that we began with in Chapter 1. One of the reasons that possession is precious is that when our team has the ball, the other team (at least barring some unfortunate fluke!) cannot score. Therefore, the best way to prevent the other team from scoring, is simply to take the ball away from them – to regain possession – as soon as possible after they win it.

This way of thinking about the goal of defending helps make it clear that, when the other team has the ball, every single person on our team is involved in defending. We have to work together to win the ball back. That is the point that this Chapter develops.

# 8.1 ⚽ Pressuring high

Of course, we never want to lose the ball. But we do want it to be the case that when we do lose the ball, we lose it deep in the opponent's half. (For example, we take a good, smart shot on goal, but miss, and now the other team has a goal kick. Or: we attempt a beautiful, on-the-ground, defense-splitting through-ball, but the timing isn't quite right and the other team wins it.) The reason we want to lose the ball up there, given that we will sometimes lose it, is that we are OK taking risks to try to score goals. When the ball is in our defensive end, by contrast, we want to play it safe so we don't give up goals.

But this implies that most of the time when we transition from playing offense to playing defense, that is happening in our offensive end of the field, and the players closest to the ball will actually be our forwards, wings, or midfielders.

When (especially) our forward players initiate pressure on the ball way up in our offensive end, that is called "pressuring high" or the "high press." And just as discussed in the last chapter (which focused more on pressuring *low*, i.e., defending in more emergency-like situations in our *defensive* end of the field), when you pressure high, you should always do so with a purpose. But the purposes can be slightly different up high than they are down low.

For example, we stressed in Chapter 7 that the number one, non-negotiable priority, when you are pressuring the ball in your defensive end, is to not let the ball-carrier get past you. In a high press situation, you still certainly don't want to just let the ball-carrier dribble right by you. But if she does get by you, it's not the same type of disaster as it is on the defensive end of the field. So you should be a little more aggressive at trying to actually steal the ball away from the ball-carrier when you are applying a high press. You can still keep a cushion of space between you and her, and even drift backwards as she moves forward with the ball to maintain that cushion. But maybe the cushion can be one or two yards instead of three or four, and you should feel free to pounce sooner, instead of waiting patiently for that perfect opportunity to stab in and try to steal the ball or poke it away. If you can hassle her and generate even a 50% chance of stealing the ball, go for it, knowing that all your teammates are behind you in defensive support if you don't get it.

The secondary purposes that you can be trying to achieve, even while applying generic vanilla pressure, can also be a little different up high. For example, you will still want to "force" the ball-carrier into a certain direction as we discussed in Chapter 7. But which way to force might be a little different.

When we're pressuring low, in our defensive end, we would almost always prefer to have the ball be out wide, rather than in the middle, for the simple reason that it's hard to score from out wide. So we generally want to let ball-carriers dribble (or pass) out toward the sidelines, and prevent them from dribbling (or passing) toward the middle of the field. That is, we want to force to the outside.

But when we are pressuring high, in our offensive end, the areas of the field near the sidelines are friendlier for them than for us. They, too, have read Chapter 3 and therefore want width! We, on the other hand, would really prefer that, if the other team is going to have the ball for a while, they keep it in the center of the field in front of the goal they are defending. That way, if and when we do eventually win the ball back, our getting the ball is dangerous for them and fantastic for us, because we have it in the middle of the field, right in front of the goal, and can maybe create a quick goal-scoring opportunity.

So it is often a good idea, when you are pressuring high, to force the player with the ball back toward the middle (rather than forcing to the outside as you would generally want to do on the defensive end). See Figure 8A for a simple example.

This idea of "forcing middle" up high is the core of many teams' high pressing strategy. It is perfectly legitimate and effective. But I think the opposite strategy also has merit, so I will describe it too. While it is often the case that there is a lot of space out wide, and often the best way of moving the ball downfield is by getting it to a winger who can move it forward through that space, it is also the case that the sideline can be used effectively as a free, additional defender. That is, it can be possible to generate turnovers by luring the other team to play the ball out wide (say, to an outside back) and then applying pressure that forces the ball-carrier up against the sideline and traps her there.

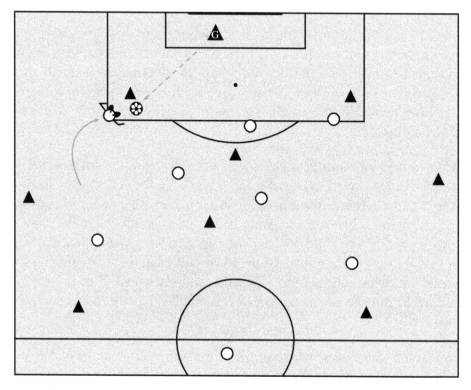

*Figure 8A: An example of a "force middle" type high press: as the black triangle goalie plays the ball out to the right back (from a goal kick, say), you apply pressure that prevents the right back from dribbling or passing out wide. Note in particular that you smartly take a curved path toward the player with the ball. This allows you to cut off her option of passing to her right wing earlier, and also accomplishes another vitally important secondary purpose that we will discuss in the next section.*

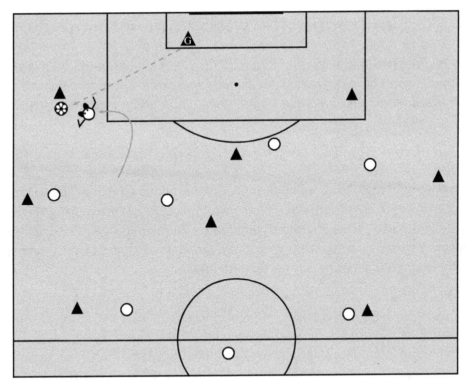

*Figure 8B: An example of a "force wide" type high press: as the black triangle goalie plays the ball out to the right back (from a goal kick, say), you apply pressure that prevents her from playing it back to the goalie or the central defender, in effect trapping her up against the sideline. It is crucial here that a midfielder behind you is preventing a pass to the black triangle right wing, who is just in front of, and the obvious passing outlet for, the right back as she gets pressed up against the sideline. And note again your excellent curved run-up, which allows you to start preventing the right back from passing the ball back toward the center much earlier, before you even get near the ball.*

This approach to initiating pressure, up high, to try to generate turnovers, is shown in Figure 8B.

## 8.2 ⊙ Communicate with your run-ups

I said before that, when you pressure high, you can take more risks and try to actually win the ball (rather than making absolutely sure that the ball-carrier doesn't dribble past you). Still, you can rarely generate a turnover all by yourself.

No matter how it is implemented exactly, the possibility of creating a turnover with the high press crucially involves not just you, the person applying pressure to the ball, but also your teammates behind you. Consider, for example, the situation shown in Figure 8B. You're doing a nice job preventing the black triangle right back from dribbling or passing toward the center of the field. In effect, you trapped her up against the sideline so that her only option is to dribble or pass forward, along the sideline.

But this situation is only problematic for the black triangles because the way forward, along the sideline, is also blocked. Your teammate, the white circles' left winger, has done a really nice job of getting into the one place the black triangle defender desperately needs to play the ball. If that teammate of yours weren't there – if, for example, she were 20 yards deeper, or 20 yards closer to the center of the field – your high pressure would accomplish nothing. The right back would just play the pass to the right winger in front of her. So it is really only by working together, in concert, that the two of you can generate a turnover.

How does that turnover come? There are several possibilities. One is that the right back, seeing no good passing option in front of her, tries to dribble past you (either forward, or back toward her own goal) and you manage to steal the ball off her feet. You're the hero! Another possibility is that the right back, knowing that trying to dribble out of trouble on defense is dangerous, tries to force a pass to an insufficiently-open teammate such as her right wing. In that case, maybe your teammate, the left wing, just intercepts the pass. She's the hero! Or maybe the right back just caves in to the pressure and boots the ball downfield to nobody in particular, and your center back easily picks it up. The point is, no matter who gets the official credit for the turnover in the stat sheet, this kind of turnover is always a genuine team effort.

The same point, obviously, applies if you are instead implementing the "force middle" type of high press. Take another look at Figure 8A and in particular how your teammates behind you are arranged. Your left wing, who in Figure 8B was all the way out on the sideline blocking off the pass to the black triangle winger, is in this other situation much nearer the middle of the field, blocking off passes to the black triangle *center* midfielders. And all of your other teammates have also shifted their positions, pushing up and in aggressively on the right hand side of the field. Your teammates, that is, are *trusting* that your "force middle" will actually be effective, so they have prepared for the ball to go back into the center and/or to the right side of the field and they're ready to intercept almost any pass in that direction.

But here is the crucial question. How did your teammates know to adjust their positions *that* way? How did they know whether you were going to "force middle" or instead "force wide"?

One possible answer is: your team just always does this the same way, so they know what to expect. If that's the case, that's great. But the point I want to make here is that this isn't necessary. You can communicate, on the fly, to your teammates behind you, which way you are going to force (and thereby tell them which way they need to shift so that the team as a whole is in the best position to generate a turnover) in the way you run up toward the ball-carrier to apply pressure.

That is the additional virtue of the curved run-ups that I pointed out previously. If you approach the ball as in Figure 8A, your teammates, who are all behind you and able to see what you are doing, receive a clear signal that you are going to force the ball back toward the middle/right, and that they should therefore shift up and to the right and get ready to intercept the forthcoming attempted outlet pass. On the other hand, if you instead approach the ball as shown in Figure 8B, it is a clear signal to your teammates that you are going to force the ball toward the sideline on the left, and so they should all shift up and left.

Figure 8C shows all of this in one "big picture" view. The details of each player's movements should maybe not be taken too seriously. Exactly how far, and in what direction, each player should shift in response to the direction of the high press will depend on many factors including: the exact location of the ball, each team's formation, each player's individual speed and size, the speed and skill of the ball-carrier, etc. Instead, the point to focus on here

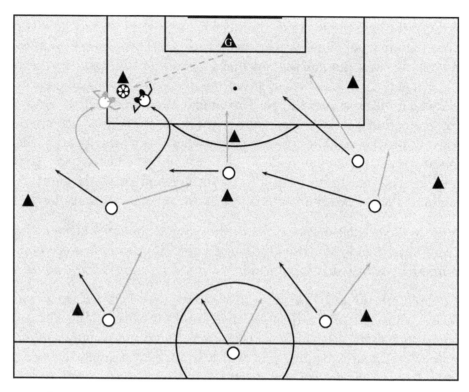

*Figure 8C: The black triangle goalie plays the ball out to the right back. As you move toward the new ball-carrier to initiate pressure, the shape of your run-up tells your teammates behind you which way you are going to force and how they should adjust their own positions to maximize the chances of creating a turnover. Note the departure from the usual black/gray color-coding here. In this Figure, the black arrows show how your teammates might move in the case (also shown in black) that your run-up signals "force wide". The gray arrows show how your teammates might move if you instead signal "force middle" with your run-up.*

is just the big picture fact that *everybody reacts* to what you do.

Generating a turnover when the other team has the ball on your offensive end is a true team effort.

## 8.3 ⊛ Pushing up in the back

I want to highlight a particular way in which the team effort just described can break down and fail.

Sometimes players have the following mindset: "If I'm a defender, then my job happens on the defensive end of the field, so I should stay back there." But this is completely wrong, and leads to a couple of really unfortunate results.

One of those unfortunate results is that, when our team starts building an attack out of our own defensive end – when we successfully maintain possession and move the ball forward into our offensive end – defenders with this mindset tend to check out and hang back, as shown in Figure 8D.

This means that the defenders are completely unavailable to be involved in the attack. In particular, they offer no helpful support (e.g., backwards-diagonal passing options) to the midfielders. As far as our attack is concerned, it is as if those three players had walked completely off the field for a quick snack break. We are at a three-person disadvantage and there is almost no way we can score. So we will almost certainly turn the ball over to the black triangles.

And that is when the second unfortunate result of the defenders' inexcusably deep positioning rears its ugly head.

Suppose, for example, we lose the ball over on the right side of the field, and the black triangles' left back ends up with it. Our team immediately shifts into "high press" mode, with our forward forcing toward the outside and the midfielders taking up appropriately aggressive positions as shown in Figure 8E.

Do you see the problem? Our forward and midfielders have, respectively, trapped the ball-carrier up against the sideline and taken away all of her short passing options. But the two black triangle forwards, near the center line, are completely wide open! There's no white circles player within 30 yards of either of them. So the ball-carrier, if she is even remotely competent, will simply play the ball in the air down to the midfield area where one of her forwards can easily collect it.

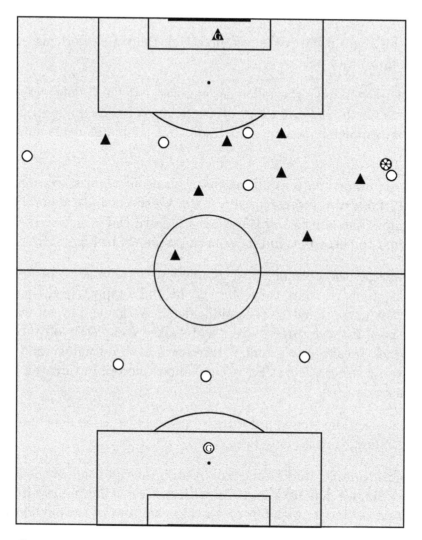

*Figure 8D: The white circles have moved the ball forward into the offensive end, but the defenders (thinking, quite wrongly, that their work is done) hang way back. This makes them totally unable to be involved in the play, and means that we are at a serious numbers disadvantage. It is therefore extremely likely that we will fail to score and instead just end up turning the ball back over to the black triangles. And, when we inevitably do that, the positioning of the white circles defenders only causes further trouble.*

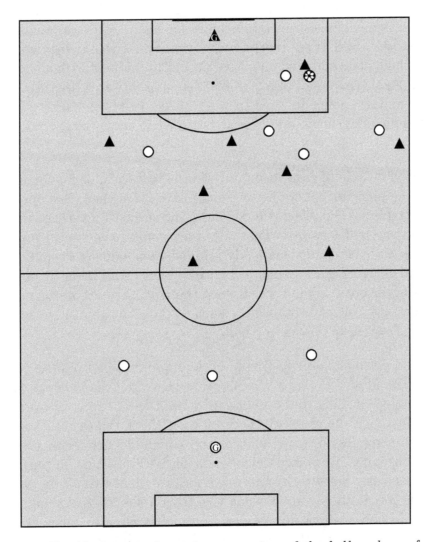

*Figure 8E: The black triangles gain possession of the ball and our forwards and midfielders immediately transition to defense: our forward applies wide-forcing pressure on the ball, and the midfielders move to block off all the short outlet passes. But unfortunately, the defenders are (still) way too far back, as disengaged now from our team's defensive efforts as they were previously from our team's offensive efforts. And in particular, their positioning gives the black triangles an easy and free outlet: they can just play the ball long, to one of their two forwards who are wide open near the midfield line.*

It's of course true that when the black triangles get the ball in this situation, it is not an immediate scoring opportunity for them. After all, we have three defenders back. Still, it's a pretty good situation for them: they completely broke our high press and now they have the ball at midfield with no immediate pressure. Furthermore, all of our midfielders and forwards are in pretty bad positions and are going to have to work hard to recover backwards as the black triangle midfielders (and defenders!) push forward to try to develop an attack.

Maybe we'll be able to stop them and win the ball back, or maybe not. But, you see, the point is that we never should have given them this opportunity in the first place. Our defenders should have pushed forward earlier, when we moved the ball forward. That way they could have stayed involved in our attack and thereby dramatically improved our odds of keeping the ball longer and generating a legitimate chance to score. And then, by pushing up and staying involved while we still have the ball, they are automatically in good aggressive defensive positions – such as those shown in Figures 8A, 8B, and 8C – if/when we do lose the ball.

Why would defenders ever just hang back and disengage from the play as in Figures 8D and 8E? Perhaps it is just that they are exhausted, or lazy, and hence unable/unwilling to move forward when the ball goes forward. To the extent that that's the problem, the solution is (in the short term) to replace them with some less fatigued players and (in the longer term) to work on their conditioning. But often defenders hang back like this on purpose, not just because they are too tired to move forward. They think, in particular, that their job is simply to prevent the other team from scoring, a thing which could only realistically happen from pretty close to the goal they are defending. So, in effect, they hang around at the job-site and just wait until their job (as they understand it) needs to be done.

But this is another team-killing misconception. The disengaged defender thinks that her job is to challenge for the ball only in a certain area of the field. She wants to win the ball back for her team, but she fails to understand (or remember) how teams actually generate turnovers. By staying so far back, and leaving the other team's forwards wide open at midfield, she gives the opposing team an easy free outlet and hence lets them keep the ball in a situation where we could and should have been able to win it back.

Another rationale I've sometimes heard defenders give for hanging way back and disengaging from the play is that they are worried they are slower than the other team's forwards. They think that, to prevent the other team's forward from just dribbling past them after they get the ball, they – the supposedly slow defenders – need to give the forwards a 20-yard cushion.

But this is completely backwards. A speedier opponent will have a much easier time getting around you if you give her 20 yards of space to accelerate to top speed. You're much more likely to prevent her from going forward if you're right on her back, challenging for the ball, the instant she receives it. But even that grossly understates the point. If you're tightly marking – or standing in front of – the other team's forward at midfield, you can easily prevent the pass from coming – or getting – to her in the first place, and your relative speeds never even enter into the discussion!

How should the disengaged defender reconceptualize her job description so that she's helping, instead of killing, her team? Terminologically, it might help if she thinks of herself as a "back" instead of a "defender". Her job is to provide a layer of depth behind the midfielders, on both offense and defense, and on both ends of the field. So when the ball and the midfielders go forward, she needs to move forward with them, in order to continue to offer vertical support. She is a crucial part of our attack – just a part that happens to be near the back of our overall shape.

And then, when our team loses the ball up high, the defenders – the backs – are an absolutely essential part of our concerted, whole-team effort to re-establish possession by simultaneously pressuring the ball and eliminating all viable passing options.

Incidentally, all of this applies to the goalie as well.

Goalies should move forward and provide deep but still-meaningful support to the attack when we have the ball and should be ready to step forward and win the ball if the other team tries to play it long, into the space behind our backs. No, we usually don't want our goalie up at midfield. But goalies should typically play well above the top of the penalty area when our team has the ball in the offensive end!

## 8.4 ⚽ Always engaged

We have previously discussed how it is crucially important, for our offensive attack, for every player on the team to stay constantly engaged, both physically and mentally. You cannot just sit back and "watch the show" when somebody else on your team has the ball. Instead, you need to be continuously working to get yourself open for the next pass (or the pass after that) and anticipating what the player with the ball is going to do next and how the defense is going to react and how you can give yourself a head-start, now, to take advantage of the situations that will develop.

The same principle applies just as much when the other team has the ball. As we have been discussing, you can never let yourself "check out" and disengage from the play.

Defending – i.e., winning the ball back from the other team when they have it – is a whole-team project. Forwards are often – forwards are *ideally* – our first defenders, and every other player on the team must be mentally engaged to see which direction the first defender is pressuring the ball and then move, in reaction, as needed to take away the ball-carrier's passing options and generate a turnover. Everybody has to be fully involved, no matter what position they are playing and no matter where the ball is on the field, for it to work.

## 8.5 ⚽ Pressuring fast

We have been discussing how our team, by working together, can generate a turnover when the other team tries to play it out from their defensive end. Figure 8C, for example, showed two ways that our team might respond, defensively, when the other team plays a goal kick out to their right back. In practice, the other team's goal kick is a great opportunity for us to apply a high pressing defense, because the stoppage of play gives us time to get into a good shape – such as that shown in Figure 8C – from which we can adjust appropriately depending on which way the ball comes out and which way the first defender forces.

But many turnovers do not come with such stoppages of play. When we lose the ball "on the fly," we have to transition to whole-team defending immediately, without the breath-catching and shape-correcting pause associated with a stoppage of play such as a goal kick. All other things being equal, this makes it harder for us: it may not be immediately clear which of our players should step to the ball to apply pressure, our backs and midfielders might not be in ideal positions from which to move to cut off passing options, etc.

But all other things are *not* equal. The other team is also, to use the technical term, discombobulated: they are probably way more bunched up near the middle of the field (or near one sideline) than they would ideally like to be when they have the ball (just because that's what naturally happens when your team is defending), they are probably lacking in both width and depth, many of their players are probably still facing strange directions that prevent them from seeing how they should move to re-establish the desired level of combobulation, etc.

The point is that even though, in the moments just following our loss of possession, our team is not in the ideal shape to apply a perfectly orchestrated whole-team defense, we should still initiate our press *immediately*. We can often take advantage of the other team's temporary disorganization and win the ball back in the first few seconds after we've lost it.

That is, as soon as we lose the ball, somebody – ideally, whoever is closest to the ball, but there's no point wasting time worrying about exactly who that should be – should just seize the initiative and immediately pressure the new ball-carrier. Often, if she acts fast enough, this first defender can steal the ball right back from the ball-carrier's feet, because the ball-carrier didn't expect to have the ball, is facing some crazy direction, and hasn't had time to look up to identify passing options yet. But this doesn't always happen and so the first defender should, in addition to just hassling the ball-carrier and trying to steal the ball, also pressure with a purpose – for example, forcing the ball carrier in a certain direction – to which our other players can respond by trying to cut off outlet passes into that direction.

We can put it this way. The other team also probably understands the points we discussed back in Chapter 3. They, too, will want width (and the easier passing opportunities that flow from it) when they gain possession of the ball.

So let's try to steal the ball back before they have a chance to spread out.

That is, let's implement the same defensive strategy that we've been discussing since the beginning of this Chapter, but in a slightly more chaotic, improvised, and *urgent* way.

## 8.6 ☻ Overview

We want to score goals so we can win games. But scoring goals is not something any one player can do, by herself, while everybody else stands around watching. (Not consistently, anyway, and not against decent competition.) Scoring goals must instead be a whole-team project, whose successful completion requires holding possession for long stretches, moving up the field together as a unit, passing the ball around quickly to stretch and distort the defense, and waiting patiently for the right moment to strike.

Winning games, however, also requires that we prevent the other team from scoring. The best way to do this is to not let them have the ball. Possession, that is, is not only the fundamental means of achieving the basic offensive aim of scoring goals; it is also the fundamental means of achieving the basic defensive aim of preventing the other team from scoring goals.

Possession really is precious!

Defense is the science of generating turnovers. And the way to generate turnovers is, in principle, simple: the first defender should force the ball into a certain direction, while all of her teammates work together to block off all viable options in that direction. We leave the other team no way out and – one way or another – we end up with the ball.

It really is that simple in principle. In practice, though, every single person on our team has to be fully engaged to make it work. When the other team has the ball, and we are defending, we must "be as one" – we must, in short, D as one.

# CHAPTER 9

---

# The Beginning

*"Sort yourself out first, that has always been my philosophy."*

- Johan Cruyff

Congratulations, you have reached the end of this book! I hope it has enriched your understanding of some of soccer's fundamental concepts, and I hope this knowledge will be a useful tool in your quest to become a better soccer player.

But knowledge is only a tool, so this end is really only the beginning. There is still a lot of work to do, to develop your skills and technique, and to learn to consistently implement, with your own team, the ideas we have been discussing.

But I know you'll do great if you work hard, have fun, stay engaged, and – most importantly – play with your brain!

# Appendix for Coaches

*"By making it more and more complicated we have lost track of the basics."*

- Johan Cruyff

I only returned to the game of soccer, as a volunteer parent coach and amateur player, about 5 years ago, after something like two decades away. The things I have learned about the game since then – that is, the ideas I wrote about in this book – have unquestionably made me both a better player and a better coach.

But, boy, it sure would have been useful to have understood all of this stuff 30 years ago, when I was playing in high school, or even 5 years ago, when I first started coaching! My hope is that this book will help give current players, and other beginning coaches, the kind of head-start I wish had been available to me.

The whole book so far has been aimed at players, so let me close with some advice specifically for my fellow coaches.

First, you just have to be patient. Even once you develop a clear sense of the direction you want to take your team, my experiece is that it takes years before you really see them start to play in a beautiful, coordinated, unstoppable way. It helps, of course, to start early and to keep the messaging as simple and as consistent as possible. But it still takes time. Indeed, it can be frustrating how long it takes. But if you are patient and keep it fun, they will stick with it until they get it, and when that happens it is wonderful.

Second, I think the biggest mistake beginning coaches make is to try to do too much. In terms of practice planning especially, it is easy and tempting to jump from one topic to another, plucking almost randomly from the millions of detailed session plans that are available online. So, for example, this Tuesday we focus on shooting with 4 different drills, then Thursday we're working on throw-ins, then next Tuesday we work on stepovers and other dribbling moves, and so on. But this is just too disjointed, too incoherent, and too disconnected from the actual game of soccer. The kids at best only half-got whatever the point was supposed to be with throw-ins on Thursday, and then we're on to some other unrelated next thing. Whole seasons can go by in which your dozens of training sessions add up to essentially nothing, and the kids don't really progress.

Instead, I think, you have to pick just a small number of basic activities, which are game-realistic in terms of requiring decision-making in the face of pressure, and use them (with small modifications here and there) over and over again, so the kids can actually develop certain essential skills. I would say, for example, that about 90% of my team's practice session time, in recent years, has been spent on just three kinds of activities (and two of them are arguably the same thing): keepaway, rondos, and small-sided games.

Let me briefly describe what these are and how I use them.

## Keepaway

Keepaway is just what it sounds like: the kids are divided into two teams and each team tries to maintain possession, i.e., keep the ball away from the other team, for as long as possible.

Other than the fact that there are no goals, this is quite similar to real soccer. It is a direct and obvious way to convey the value of possession, and, by playing it, kids have to figure out how to successfully implement many of the ideas discussed in the book: spreading out so there are open passing options and so that they have time to decide what to do next when they get it; moving into seams between defenders and moving toward the ball to receive passes; facing the space when they receive the ball so they can see what's coming and where they should send it next; working together, as one, on defense to generate turnovers; etc.

The fact that there are no goals means you don't have to constantly fight against the kids with the tendency to always dribble forward and try to score (no matter how many defenders are in the way). Some kids will still hold the ball too long, to be sure, and you can push back against that, but it is much easier to help them see how pointless and counter-productive this is, when there is no particular place the ball is supposed to go. Indeed, the fact that there is no forward and no backward (just a big space) makes keepaway great for encouraging kids to just pass, as quickly as possible, to the most open teammate, no matter what direction they happen to be in. Kids' inherent resistance to passing backwards is neutralized when there is no forward or backward.

Keepaway is also competitive and fun. Kids love doing it, and it's helping them develop fundamental game-applicable soccer skills. So I say, let them do it, frequently, at your practices.

Here are some ways you can tweak/modify the games to adjust the difficulty level and keep things interesting. If kids are having trouble holding possesion for more than a pass or two in an even-numbered game, introduce one or two "neutral" (i.e., "all-time offense") players. Then the team with the ball always has a numbers advantage and should be able to have more success. In another fun variation, there are three teams, with two of them working together to try to keep it away from the third. (The team on defense at any moment is the team of the player who most recently gave the ball away to the previous defensive team.) This game will keep them on their toes, physically and mentally. To encourage kids to work on playing *faster*, you can award a point for each successful one-touch pass. Whichever team accumulates more points in a certain time period is the winner. You can also introduce special zones into keepaway games. For example, make a small square with cones in the center of the area, and award a point to a team any time they can complete a pass into that area and then get the ball back out again. This encourages players to make runs, into the target area, when they don't have the ball, and requires other players to pass the ball around and keep possession, while also watching out for the right moment to try to pass into the target zone. Or, put "end-zones" on two opposite sides of the area and award a point any time a team can move the ball, without losing it, from one end-zone to the other.

# Rondos

Rondos are really just small keepaway games, but with a certain structure that makes them perfect for developing several aspects of technique and skill.

The simplest rondo, which I recommend starting with and doing every day at practice for at least several years, is simply 4-v-1 keepaway, with the four offensive players each living on one edge of a (roughly 10 or 15 yard) square area. The offensive players are allowed to pass to either adjacent player (but not across the middle) and should be required to settle the ball and then make the next pass (with the inside of the appropriate foot, of course) with just two touches. The defender runs around in the middle trying to win the ball, at which point he gets to trade places with whoever gave the ball up to him. It looks like this:

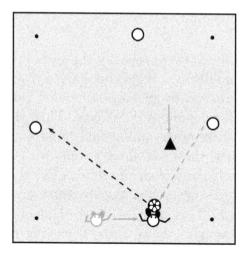

Each time one of the offensive players gets the ball, he has to settle it and then decide between his two passing options (namely, sending it right back to the person who just passed it to him, or sending it to the player on his other side) based on where the defender is. This activity requires kids to develop better and quicker decision-making, accurate settling and passing skills, and good receiving technique. (Note that although offensive players are restricted to one edge of the square, they can and should slide, from side to side, along that edge, both to get open, as needed, for a teammate who is under some pressure, and also to make sure they are always receiving the ball correctly, with the back foot, even when the incoming pass is not perfect.)

The 3-v-1 rondo is also very interesting and valuable. Here, the three offensive players are free to move around on the inside of (rather than just along the perimeter of) a square area, as they try to keep it away from the defender. Players should quickly discover that, whenever one of their teammates passes the ball to another teammate, the player who wasn't involved in that pass needs to yell with his legs to provide a good next passing option. The player and the ball often get to a corner at roughly the same moment, so the player has to work hard to arrive at the spot, turn to face the space, and receive the ball correctly (with the back foot), so he can make the next pass quickly and accurately. Here's a picture:

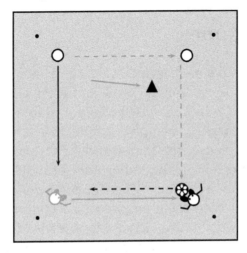

You can explore more complicated rondos when kids start to master the basics.

For example, the 4-v-2 rondo is just like the 4-v-1 but with a somewhat bigger square and two defenders in the middle. The offensive players can now be allowed to pass through the middle to the player on the opposite side, and, in particular, can score a point by completing a pass that splits – goes between – the two defenders. This encourages the offensive players to constantly seek the (moving) seams. Generating turnovers (and avoiding embarrassing splits) requires the two defenders to D as one. To help encourage this defensive teamwork, let both defenders swap out of the middle whenever either one of them gets the ball. This helps them see that, no matter who happens to get the ball, the turnover was jointly-produced.

You can also add a 5th offensive player, who is free to move around the interior of the square (so, a 5-v-2, but with 5=4+1, i.e., four on the edges and one in the middle). To be effective, that 5th offensive player, in the middle, has to do a lot of the more complicated central-midfielder things we discussed in Chapter 5: getting open in the seam behind the defenders and receiving the ball on the half-turn (to move it away from pressure) when it comes, but also recognizing when the seam is closing and moving toward the ball if that's what's needed to provide an emergency option.

I hope you can see how rondos provide a simple but still game-realistic "sandbox" for working on literally every point covered in the book.

## Small-sided games

This is also just as simple as it sounds. Let the kids play soccer. Get some small portable pop-up (e.g., "pugg") goals and bring them to every practice. If you have a team of 12-16 kids, break them into four teams and have two 3v3 games going in parallel. Simply playing 3v3 is a great way for kids to learn, through experience, the importance of triangles, width, and depth (on both offense and defense), the importance of moving to get open when they don't have the ball, and many other fundamental concepts. If there are extra players, you can keep them engaged by letting them be neutral (all-time-offense) wingers who are restricted to a sideline. Or get rid of the goals and let teams score by passing to a target player who lives on the endline.

You can quickly transition from two parallel small-sided games to one bigger game by simply removing the cones that separated the two small fields. If the two small fields had pop-up goals on both ends, now your big field will have two widely-separated goals on each end. That's great – leave them there! Games like this (with two separate targets on each end) give the kids a great opportunity to learn to recognize when the way forward on one side is clogged, and they need to switch the point of attack.

As with the keepaway games, you can add one or more neutral (all-time-offense) players to any game to help the offense have more success. If teams are turning the ball over too often, you can help them remember that possession is precious by letting them score points not just by putting the ball into (one of) the goal(s), but also by completing a certain number of consecutive passes.

Probably my favorite mini-game is to just play half-field soccer, with a full- (or nearly full-) sized team defending the full-sized goal on the end of the field, and another team (with fewer people) defending two small goals on the midfield line, one near each sideline. The team defending the big goal gets to practice working the ball out of the back, with something like a full-sized team and real assigned positions. Scoring a goal (in one of the small goals in the wing areas near midfield) is closely related to getting the ball to a winger, with space to go forward, in a real game. (I sometimes require that, in order for the team defending the big goal to score in one of the little goals, every player except the goalie has to be forward, beyond some designated "midfield" line. This trains the defenders/goalie to move forward with the ball and stay engaged, so you never have to see the horror of Figure 8D in games.)

In this half-field game, the team defending the two small goals has fewer players and so has to work a little harder (just as forwards and midfielders have to work hard in the high press). But they are motivated to wor hard by the fact that if and when they do win the ball, they get to try to score on the real full-sized goal.

The roles can also be reversed: the full-sized team (minus the goalie) can attack the full-sized goal, while the team with somewhat fewer players defends the big goal and tries to score with a quick counter-attack on one of the two mini-goals at midfield. This can help the full-sized team develop a feeling for patiently possessing the ball in the offensive end, working to create a good goal-scoring opportunity by moving the ball around quickly.

So, if you only get half of a field to practice on and/or there aren't enough players for a full-field game, don't despair: playing half-field is a great way to let the kids learn to implement the ideas from the book in a way that feels, to them, like a "real game."

* * *

Notice that in all of the practice activities I've described, every kid is fully and actively engaged at all times. In particular, they are continuously making open-ended decisions about where to move, which way to face, which of two possible passes to make next, at what angle to apply pressure, etc. I deliberately and systematically avoid – and urge you to also avoid – wasting time on "drills" where kids are being told exactly what to do, and then standing around in lines waiting for their turn to do it. Actions practiced in this way simply do not translate into improved performance in games, and for a very simple reason: in games, nobody else can tell you exactly what to do when.

Kids do need to develop certain basic individual skills. But you can encourage them to practice their dribbling, footwork, juggling, and shooting at home, on their own, so your precious time together at practice can be spent on more interactive, cognitively-challenging activities. At practice, whatever specific technical skill or concept you want your kids to be working on, find a way to have them work on it in the context of a game-like activity (such as a rondo or other keepaway game) or just a real (maybe small-sided) game.

Why?

Because soccer is a game you play with your brain.

# Acknowledgements

Lots of people helped make this book exist and helped make it better. First, my wife (Sarah) and kids (Finn and Tate) and even my parents (Carol and Steve) read and edited drafts, provided feedback, and generally put up with me while I became temporarily obsessed with this project. Sarah Auerbach and Marshall Nelson provided invaluable help on the publishing and legal fronts, respectively. Sarah Heim, Chris Sorensen, Tom Duffy, Dave Lively, Chris Hayhurst, Jhon Giraldo, Dave Marlin, Matt Card, Pranay Parikh, David Sanford and Michael Filas all gave helpful constructive feedback on early drafts. Thanks to all!

Thanks also to Dave M, Pranay P, Rei M, and Andrew (from the team I coach) for the book review blurbs that I used on the back cover – and also to the several other people who provided blurbs that, unfortunately, I wasn't able to squeeze in.

Seth Gregory designed a beautiful and clever cover and was a pleasure to work with. Thank you, Seth, for being so responsive and creating the perfect piece of art for this project.

This book would certainly not exist if my youth soccer coaches (Kenny Bensinger, Tim Flint, Paul Henden, and several others) hadn't volunteered so much time and positive energy. Thanks for helping me learn and keeping it fun!

Finally, thanks to *you*, dear reader, for sticking with the book all the way to the end. If you found it to be a valuable resource, you can help spread the good word by lending your copy to a friend, posting about it on social media, or writing a review at your favorite online bookstore.

CPSIA information can be obtained
at www.ICGtesting.com
Printed in the USA
LVHW101155040520
654954LV00013B/1427

9 781734 528008